EXPLOSIVE ECOMMERCE GROWTH

Take your webshop from average to exceptional and enjoy exponential growth along the way

NUNO MORGADINHO

K
N
O
W
N

TESTIMONIALS

"We experienced a much better performance and user experience yesterday than on a normal Wednesday. Overall, the webshop has been three times faster while serving 10% more pages."

NICOLAI, CTO @ FRESH.LAND

"What a day, guys! I can't thank you enough for all your hard work on this."

DEBORA GRILO, HEAD OF BRAND AND CREATIVE @ UNBABEL.COM

"Per usual, you're so great! Thank you for all of the updates!"

RACHAEL NEEL, MARKETING EXECUTIVE @ MONDAGO.COM

PREFACE

Selling online can be a lot of fun and also very rewarding. Today, the size of the global market is already the biggest it's ever been thanks to the reach of the internet. We can sell almost whatever we like to thousands of people. I imagine, if you're reading this book, it's because you've already experienced the thrill of selling online[1] and you know how exhilarating it is. If you sell internationally then you've already reached quite an important step in your ambitions to grow the business. But you know there's more – a lot more – and you're still looking for the 'yellow brick road' that will get you there.

This book is not a 'how to attain your first clients step-by-step guide'. If you are new to eCommerce or are looking for a complete A-Z book on the subject, I recommend reading *Digital Business and E-Commerce Management* by Dave Chaffey.[2]

In writing this book I have made some assumptions, namely:

- You already have clients.

- Your webshop is built on WordPress/ WooCommerce.

- You have (or want to hire soon) an internal tech team or third-party agency to carry out the necessary work outlined in this book.

- You want to go to the next level with your webshop.

- Your business model is solid and you have already proved that your business can gain traction.

- You know your webshop could be delivering significantly better results.

- You are ready to scale to the next level.

The good news is what you're about to read makes this exactly the right book to help you precisely plan that journey towards achieving explosive eCommerce growth, because it's aimed at people like you, be that the founder, or part of the leadership team, of an online business which is looking to:

- grow in existing markets

- expand into new markets

- reach mass market

- be the lighthouse of your industry.

Every piece of advice given in the context of this book is based on my first-hand experience – I only highlight a problem/gap if I've experienced the problem myself, or if I've seen a client experience it and we can measure the business impact after we've solved it. I also only offer advice or recommendations that I've seen working, fixing or minimising such problems/gaps.[3]

I'm the founder and managing director at WidgiLabs, a global digital agency that specialises in eCommerce. My international client portfolio includes brands such as Forbes and Vodafone, amongst others. I've also worked with over 100 different clients across a variety of business sectors, from established brands to start-ups, including Uniplaces, which is now an international case study. Working with the best designers and developers, I've helped create numerous webshops that now receive millions of page views per month. In Portugal, I worked on the launch of two of the biggest media installations for Observador and ECO, both of which won awards.

I am passionate about product design and helping brands deliver the best possible online experience for customers. For that reason, I love to explore the huge potential that digital technology offers and, in doing so, I also love to help business owners close the gap between where they are now in their early-to-mid stages of growth and their vision of future explosive success.

CONTENTS

HOW TO
USE THIS BOOK

This book is designed specifically with CEOs and leadership teams in mind whose webshop is built on WordPress and employs WooCommerce. It features my eCommerce Foundations Roadmap that serves as a logical step-by-step guide to cover the critical building blocks required to optimise potential and lead to explosive growth.

Its aim is to piece the eCommerce puzzle together so that everyone on your leadership team is aligned and able to view the wider strategic vision picture. Use it as a checklist to ask the right questions of your internal SMEs and external partners at the right time without needing detailed knowledge of complex technical elements. Each step will empower you to lead your webshop's growth plan from the front.

A successful implementation of the Foundations Roadmap requires that each step is followed in the order I've laid out. If you are tempted to skip any of the chapters because you're keen to quickly drive sales/increase conversions, then I would urge you to please consider otherwise.

Use this book to discover what matters when it comes to becoming more valuable in the marketplace with your eCommerce webshop. The learnings and insight I share will:

- educate you on the 5 key areas every eCommerce webshop needs to excel in

- provide you with a solid roadmap of what you need to do next

- enable you to make better decisions

- invest in the areas where you'll see the most return

- help you to choose the right partner to assist you in achieving your goals

- enable you to generate more revenue and profit.

Finally, take advantage of the free-to-use self-assessment tool in the last chapter to measure your current position, and repeat the exercise on a regular basis to measure your webshop's progress.

Now is the time to go from good to truly remarkable and to aim for that explosive eCommerce growth you've dreamed of.

INTRODUCTION: THE ECOMMERCE OPPORTUNITY

NOW IS SUCH A GOOD TIME FOR ECOMMERCE

While some traditional sectors of our economy struggle for survival, eCommerce has experienced a huge surge in demand. The new reality is that people have become reliant on online shopping. And while our weekly grocery shop or a book order may not have changed much in recent years, great strides in eCommerce innovation are taking place, and at a rapid pace.

For most of us, it's hard to imagine modern life without eCommerce in the many forms we use it, such as ordering goods, making a booking, purchasing a service, buying a subscription and a myriad of other things. As ingrained as eCommerce has become in our lives, it wasn't that long ago when it didn't even exist! We can trace its origins back about 40 years, when 'teleshopping' first appeared as a precursor.

The following condensed timeline below shows how eCommerce has rapidly evolved over a short period of time during which Amazon, the big success, has become one of the most valuable companies in the world:

1969	CompuServe is founded. It will go on to become what many consider to be the first true eCommerce company.
1979	Fed up with regular trips to the market, Michael Aldrich introduces the world to electronic shopping.
1982	Boston Computer Exchange becomes one of the first eCommerce platforms.
1992	Charles M. Stack launches Book Stacks Unlimited, one of the first online market-places.
1994	Netscape releases Netscape Navigator, which becomes the most prominent of the early web browsers.
1994	Jeff Bezos unveils Amazon.

1995	AuctionWeb launches. Its name will eventually be changed to eBay.
1998	PayPal revolutionises eCommerce with a secure way for webshops to accept payments.
1999	Jack Ma launches Alibaba.com, a first-of-its-kind B2C, B2B, and C2C eCommerce company.
2005	Amazon introduces flat-fee, two-day shipping through Prime.
2011	Facebook throws its hat in the eCommerce ring with sponsored stories.
2011	Stripe enters the world of online payments.
2014	Apple launches Apple Pay.
2015	Google introduces Android Pay.
2015	Cyber Monday sales reach a new record high of more than $3 billion.
2016	Alibaba sets a record with $17 billion in sales in just one day.

2017	Instagram enters the eCommerce game with shoppable posts.
2019	eCommerce sales reach $3.5 trillion.
2020	The COVID-19 pandemic boosts eCommerce to a whole new level.
2021	eCommerce worth 4 trillion globally and expected to grow to 7 trillion.

Since the early part of this century, we have witnessed countless companies making that transition to sell online, and of course Amazon, the big success, has become one of the most valuable companies in the world. And eCommerce continues to progress at a rapid pace. We could even say it's only just getting started.

Why do I make that claim? Because it's my personal conviction that we are still yet to experience a whole load more innovation in this area. I see two trends happening that sustain my conviction:

1. Global connectivity continues to soar with more and more new people becoming super-connected to the internet, for example in Asia. And with that the global digital market continues to grow.

2. Technology is also rapidly evolving in a myriad of ways that help systems be more interconnected and logistics easier that create new experiences and possibilities for users and brands.

I'm particularly excited about approaches that radically change our current eCommerce experience; for example, by mixing entertainment (social buying) or education (live commerce). Rest assured, in a not-so-near future we will say goodbye to the familiar and dull experience of buying online. We'll probably also be spending more time online, be that on the Web or the metaverse. The next 10 years will be even more dynamic than the last 40 and, as you can guess, this is set to be a golden time for eCommerce. There are lots of opportunities to be mined and, as a result, rapid growth and fast profits are a real possibility.

THE IMPACT OF AI

The arrival of AI is set to have a profound impact on the world of eCommerce. In particular, large language models (LLMs) such as ChatGPT, will offer online retailers the capability to provide personalised and interactive customer services that offer immediate assistance in response to shoppers' queries as they guide them through their purchase journey.

From a business perspective, LLMs can also help streamline inventory management and supply chain operations. By leveraging AI-powered predictive analytics, retailers can optimise inventory levels, forecast demand, and automate replenishment processes. As a result, they can minimise the risk of stock shortages, as well as reduce costs associated with stock surplus to requirements. This not only improves operational efficiency but also ensures that customers can find the products they want on demand.

Augmented by ever more sophisticated algorithms, vast amounts of customer data can already be analysed, such as browsing history, purchase patterns, and preferences, that then create targeted recommendations and personalised product suggestions. This significantly enhances the customer's shopping experience in presenting them with relevant and tailored options, and as a result, the chances of conversion are significantly increased.

Customers will become accustomed to AI technologies that allow them to interact with semi-automated virtual assistants to handle routine tasks such as order tracking, returns, and refunds. This will not only free up costly human resources, it will also ensure 24/7 customer support services that meet customers' expectations for fast responses and the ability to shop at their own convenience.

Not only can LLMs simulate natural language conversations, understand customer intent, and provide accurate and relevant information, AI technologies will further revolutionise the eCommerce landscape through advancements in visual and voice search capabilities. This will undoubtedly be yet another technological game changer that enables shoppers to find desired items more easily, even if they struggle to describe them in words. Without doubt, shoppers are set to be the main beneficiaries of the current and future implementations of AI; such enhancements that deliver a more enjoyable and easier shopping experience will ultimately lead to more satisfied and loyal customers.

Such rapid rates in technological advancements are also associated with the need for change in how we all do business and manage our operations. Of course, that's easier said than done, but change is not always easy to embrace, even less so to implement without a strategic roadmap. What frustrates me the most is that it isn't the complexities of the technology itself that stands in the way of progress; it's usually the stubborn (or at best, misguided) refusal of businesses that won't hire/work with a partner to elevate their eCommerce operations to the next level that really gets in the way of any attempt to reach for the stars. Even if they do, more often than not, they simply fail to follow through. I see them cut corners or they prioritise their attention on the wrong area instead of where it's needed most. I know this because I've seen it happen all too often.

As an eCommerce expert, I'm often approached by customers with brilliant businesses and products with a decent proven track record, but in reality (and to be blunt), they're not making nearly as much money as they should on their eCommerce sites. Some of the problems they face range from unstable/unsecured slow webshops, sub-par UI/UX, the lack of know-how to enter into new markets, combined with the inability to increase sales and the need to increase recurring revenue. They don't lack ambition; they just lack the right partner.

I'm also approached by businesses that are doing very well but have come to the conclusion that what they have in place won't get them where they want to go next. For example, when opening into new markets, improving customer satisfaction, how to facilitate data processing, automation, etc. These are all challenges that eCommerce businesses going global inevitably face. Fortunately, all these challenges can be addressed with specific strategies and tools. For every problem there is a solution.

However, I'm well aware that the majority of founders don't (or won't) ask for help. Instead, they try to move the needle by themselves but, more often than not, end up stuck just because they won't take that extra step of asking for help from a third-party expert/supplier.

One thing we all agree on is that time burns money and money is the very basic thing that keeps a business alive. Therefore, it's vital that you use our time in the best way possible to maximise our chance for success. That means you need to be really good at identifying and prioritising tasks that will prove to be the most impactful for your business's growth.

Having worked with hundreds of clients, I've witnessed far too many founders not doing this well. My top tip for improvement is to simply hire a professional supplier. You might think that I would say that, because that's what I do for a living, but in all honesty, it's really great advice.

Why? Because where you link their payment to your success criteria, a supplier will be sure to take on board the responsibility of achieving the result you want. That way, not only do you hire a supplier, but you also make sure they are in a hurry to achieve the result. Working with suppliers has several advantages in comparison to working internally, and I won't go into all of them here. I hope it is sufficient to mention that Tim Cook, before he became CEO of Apple, was its Chief Procurement Officer, and in that role he used his procurement background to make Apple what it is today.

My question, therefore, to founders is: why place unnecessary effort on your back by refusing to hire specialist professionals and, instead, decide to opt for DIY? By leveraging a procurement strategy, eCommerce founders can free themselves and become ready for the next challenge – taking on bigger competitors, expanding into new markets and growing that all important loyal customer base.

That is exactly where I step in with WidgiLabs. We've developed a method to work with such businesses and we help them succeed faster. We help those businesses achieve their true potential by upgrading everything associated with their eCommerce platform. When my team is finished, they have a world-class eCommerce site that can handle a huge volume of traffic – it's fast and secure and provides a smooth purchase experience, one which customers can use intuitively. As a result, their sales soar.

There's no quick-fix solution that achieves that level of success; it takes time and it follows a methodology that unpicks the entire sales path trajectory, piece by piece. That means going right back to the basics of the website itself. One of the first hurdles we also need to cross is to convince small businesses that they can compete with the giants in the marketplace and **still** turn exceptional profits. In fact, their very size is a highly valuable asset compared to the likes of Amazon because they rely on significantly lower operational costs. Nor are they burdened by huge infrastructural complexities, and by being 'small' they can actually create a big impact on their customers due to their ability to directly connect. Last, but not least, the ability to embrace and implement change will always be far easier to manage for a smaller eCommerce business than their behemoth competitors. Once our clients understand that they do in fact have so many advantages over their bigger rivals, then knowing how to leverage their operational flexibility and intimacy of relationships is the kick-start they need to aim towards exceeding their customer expectations. And the key to that is in creating a delightful user experience that is the sum of many parts. Not just in how it looks, but how it feels and, crucially, how it's nurtured from day one.

Small, therefore, is no less a disadvantage when it comes to adapting to and adopting technological change. It's something to be celebrated and championed in equal measures. In fact, it's often the smaller players in the market that drive change and take advantage of customers' evolving preferences, innovative ideas, ridiculously exceptional customer service and developing emerging trends that bigger players either can't see, don't care about, or can't respond to fast enough. Size is frequently the enemy of flexibility, handicapping the ability to adapt and change.

However, it's that acute awareness of where you are in relationship to the market that's required in order to fully understand:

- What's shifting around you?

- What is, or isn't, working?

- Where, and how, do you add value?

'Small' wins because essentially it has so little to lose; it embraces mistakes and is committed to long-life learning. 'Small' is willing to experiment and fail. On the other hand, 'Big' succeeds by brute force, dogma, large cash injections, erecting barriers and systematising success.

A word of caution, therefore: 'Small' destroys its only competitive advantage by attempting to emulate the bigger brands. If you try to get 'Big' by emulating what they do, it will, I am afraid to say, turn out to be a costly, if not deadly, error of judgement. Trust me when I say, be slow in abandoning the advantages of being small.

However, choosing a platform to host your webshop is no small decision. Research shows that platform selection is the most crucial aspect of an eCommerce business. Essentially, there are two models: renting vs owning.

1. Renting refers to vendor platforms for which you will pay a monthly cost.

2. Owning refers to solutions like WooCommerce. Although there will still be associated costs, the difference is you will own all the data and the infrastructure.

In fact, the possibilities when owning are open-ended and this is crucial for enabling innovation in both the front-end customer experience and also in the business back-end procedures. When using WooCommerce you jump on what I like to call the 'open-source boat'. This boat features all the brands that use WooCommerce as well as all the developers and companies around the world that contribute to its active development and continuous improvement.

Bear in mind that eCommerce often calls for rapid changes – in content, in design, in functionality or general business procedures. In terms of content, an eCommerce webshop needs to continually add updated products or product information, either as part of the regular course of business or in response to particular events in the market.

For design in general, new visuals or layouts may be needed to make the webshop more attractive or easier to use. Or, as often happens in response to customer complaints, a problem comes to light surrounding functionality or general layout that can then be quickly addressed. This is when an open-source platform such as WooCommerce comes into its own: it can easily accommodate such requests, since it's relatively easy to source freelancers and agencies that work with, and specialise in it.

Overall, open source also offers other advantages, principally autonomy since your business won't be dependent on a single vendor. It will additionally benefit from the frequent and numerous releases, packed with new features, bug fixes, security and accessibility concerns, among others. You'll also benefit from being part of a large support and development community, spread over several geographic locations and time zones and different languages. The business also has access to a whole range of extensions, addons, plugins, tutorials, discussion forums and much more than can be imagined at first glance.

Having the right people and team members will inevitably help you to get those results fast. I get what it's like for anyone starting up a business. We've all been there. It's normal for founders to be a 'jack of all trades' and tinker with the technology, either building or customising the platform on their own. Entrepreneurs are famous for knowing how to go from 0 to 1 quickly, and that's fine. But, trust me, once you get to a certain point, you'll need to start delegating tasks out to one or more of the following:

1. Internal specialists

2. Freelancers

3. Partner agencies

It's not always apparent where to start, or which option will work best for the business. Having an internal team of programmers and designers allows your business to respond to stimuli quickly and keep the business running smoothly, which may not be possible if the services are outsourced due to lack of personnel, time or urgency on the part of the contracted designers and programmers. However, it's not always feasible for every business to keep a fully internal design and programming team either because of lack of budget or lack of pressing business needs to develop their own internal team.

Freelancers tend to work only on the more generic aspects of design and programming. For instance, a webshop in need of graphics may hire an outside graphic designer to develop pictures and icons. This may also be the case for a programmer hired to implement a particular integration or functionality. The more mechanical any aspect of webshop functionality, the more likely it is to be outsourced. Thus, much programming outsourcing is geared towards back-end functionality and internal aspects that keep a webshop running smoothly behind the scenes.

On the other hand, a partner agency covering strategy, UX, design, front-end and back-end development in locations all over the world has a different focus. Their focus is on making sure the right elements are in place to support your business goals securely, reliably, and at scale, to get you where you want to go fast. It takes a special set of knowledge, experience, and collaborative energy to bring that strength to the table.

In my view, and based on my experience, one of the most important decisions you'll make after reading this book is who you select as a partner agency. Unfortunately, many founders overlook this decision and ultimately hire marketing agencies that are more suited towards building online ads than creating a remarkable and premium platform for your business.[4]

I'm definitely very proud that in all my years of working alongside top designers and developers, I've helped many clients bring new ideas to market. As a result, I've learned some important lessons that I wanted to share with you via this book because I think they will help you clarify your thoughts and allay your fears by helping you to begin to shape your strategic planning. This book represents my best knowledge to date and also my best advice that I recommend to my customers. Not only do I share many of my own insights, this book also consolidates wisdom from multiple sources, mentors and case studies.

My ultimate goal is to help executive management teams assess their current eCommerce proposition and signal what it is they need to do next in order to improve. Following my recommended eCommerce Foundations Roadmap, the 5 key areas I outline will be all that you need to help achieve explosive eCommerce growth for your own business.

CHAPTER 1

THE
FOUNDATIONS
ROADMAP

The Foundations Roadmap I've designed leads your business towards greater eCommerce success. Its 'step-by-step' order is deliberately planned to offer a complete picture of what's required to maximise any WooCommerce potential for growth. Here, I set out my recommended pathway that anticipates the necessary and sequential key areas that you'll need to be aware of without the need for the actual expertise itself to implement them. After all, that's where your in-house IT professionals and external consultants will play their part.

However, it would be erroneous to rely on their expertise alone in order to guarantee the desired explosion in eCommerce growth, because in all probability, they will lack sight of the overall picture themselves. I often see how people's first instincts usually lead them towards tackling the issue of increasing sales, but that approach ignores the root problems that really lie beneath the surface. Important as optimising conversions is, it's often a knee jerk response driven by a need to quickly improve. That results in deploying 'solutions' that may well return welcome short-term gains, but which over the long term fail to deliver sustainable results. If only they had confronted the root of the problem in the right place and in the correct order...

My aim when I designed the eCommerce Foundations Roadmap was to create a series of jargon-free checklists and tools to help leaders become part of the critical developmental conversations from which they often feel excluded, or under equipped for. I am convinced that when everyone talks from the same page, this results in a shared sense of purpose that then tackles the issues and resolves the problems that has held the business back. For the leader, being informed without the necessity of being the expert, is key to successful implementation that then delivers the desired strategically planned vision.

Part of the journey is to start approaching your web-shop as a product itself. Develop the ability to laterally shift your mindset from thinking about eCommerce simply as a delivery vehicle, towards it being a product that will then effectively mass deliver your goods and services into the marketplace.

You've already done the 'easy' part – starting an eCommerce business – but as you're increasingly beginning to realise, growing it at pace can be more difficult than at first imagined. Believe me when I tell you that you are not alone. I've seen this to be the case with so many businesses that began with high ambitions and great returns, only to be stalled when revenues plateau, or even fall. However, once the executive leadership understands how each area cascades into the next (and why) then the business begins to live up to expectations, and beyond. Your role, therefore, in that success, is vital.

Each of the 5 steps below will be fleshed out in greater detail, together with case studies, to demonstrate my points in jargon-free language that won't tie anyone up in technical knots. As obvious as some of the following may seem at first glance, following the road-map in the order I prescribe will unlock your business's future potential for growth. Not only do you owe this to yourself and the business, you also owe it to your customers.

STEP 1: SECURITY

To begin with I encourage you to take direct responsibility as a leader and make security your **number one priority**.

You may well be surprised that this is the first area we ask our clients to look at when perhaps their focus is aimed towards improving their sales. However, the nuts and bolts of security is an aspect that's all too easy to overlook, especially by non-tech founders. Of course, they understand that security is of great importance, but too much attention is initially directed to the website's look and product range before security is even prioritised. Instead, I think of it this way: if you filled a warehouse top to bottom with a mountain of stock intended for sale, the first thing you'd think of is not simply to lock the doors at night, but whether you have enough locks in the first place!

Working alongside your trusted IT teams and experts, dive deeply into your security protocols and practices and closely inspect every single area where vulnerabilities may exist, caused by a variety of factors that are currently unmonitored, hidden or which can be avoided. Taking this action will give the business the confidence to know:

1. Who has actual control of your webshop if it happens to go down.

2. Which of your vendors and freelance developers have access to your system passwords and client data.

3. The measures in place to prevent data leakage being manipulated elsewhere or appearing on the dark web.

Only by keeping security as your number one priority can you create the freedom and opportunity required to then grow and scale the business. And perhaps only then can you truthfully answer:

*   Is your webshop properly secure?

*   Are you sleeping well at night?

STEP 2: SPEED AND PERFORMANCE

Amazon famously discovered that every 100 milliseconds of latency delay on the network cost them 1% in sales. As an independent webshop provider operating in a competitive market, your need to stand out is key to your successful strategic sales implementation. Speed and performance are key drivers to that success.

That's because, for many eCommerce businesses, their webshop performance equates to company performance.

Therefore, understanding the complex correlative relationship between the two is key to ramping up their growth potential. If that potential isn't addressed at the earliest stage, as well as the technical requirements to accommodate it, then the business will be on the back foot at the wrong time.

Instead, I'll show you how to maximise revenue potential when customers respond to a high-profile marketing campaign and avoid cart abandonment due to a slow-performing website. Don't worry, you don't need to be the expert in the technicalities, but you do need to be aware of the significant impact this relationship between speed and performance creates.

You know you're behind the big guys, right?

STEP 3: DELIGHTFUL USER EXPERIENCE (UX)

This is very much the nuts-and-bolts axis when the webshop begins to return meaningful, visible results about how your users interact with the webshop. It's when you discover whether this is a pleasurable user experience in respect of both the content and product flow you have created. These results must be continually evaluated and acted upon where necessary, especially when design and functional barriers to conversions or knowledge-gathering are identified.

Your aim is always to ensure that when your customers enter your store it's an enjoyable process, not a source of frustration or annoyance that prompts them to abandon their interaction. That's the huge advantage of an online store over traditional bricks and mortar retail – you have the tools at hand to offer valuable insights into your customers' behaviours.

It's a mechanism that should always prompt a leadership team to ask:

- Are our customers happy with our webshop?
- Is it easy to use intuitively?
- Is it fast?

STEP 4: CAPACITY

Once you've followed the previous steps, your webshop now looks fantastic and offers a world class user experience. It's something to be proud of that reflects your brand in the digital marketplace. It shows you're prepped and primed to welcome in as many customers as possible in the anticipation that they will not only browse, but buy.

So far, so good. Or is it? Because that's not the end of the story as far as developing your webshop is concerned.

A common mistake is the failure to properly ensure that a webshop has sufficient capacity to handle any anticipated uptake in traffic. Especially following a successful marketing campaign in partnership with a high-profile social media influencer. Their power to persuade the masses to follow their recommendation and head directly to your site in order to purchase that 'must have' product is all too easily underestimated. In which case, your webshop needs to be super turbo charged **in advance** to handle that instantaneous, simultaneous rush of traffic through its doors.

The last thing your webshop needs is a log jam of customers all seeking to fill their cart, only to be confronted with that most frustrating response – the buffering circle of hell that locks them out from their purchasing pleasure. Nobody wants that, least of all you.

STEP 5: CONVERSIONS

This is the step that you've probably been most keen to read, because it will show you how to massively improve sales. However, as I've already suggested, this can only be achieved effectively when the foundations are in place that will help sustain them. I completely understand the urge to jump in straight away and create strategies to increase sales, but the single biggest error that many webshop leaders make is prioritising it above all else. Let me be frank with you: the easiest way to burn money is to focus primarily on improving conversion rates without first addressing the previous four steps in the eCommerce Foundations Roadmap. You need to make the cake first before you add the icing.

SUMMARY

The major insight I offer from the outset is in using your power of discretion by approaching the roadmap in the correct order – and that means addressing conversions last. It's the logical point in the development chain that really enables the business to mine the gold that you've dug deep for in the process to date, one that is more complex in parts than others. Collectively, they will contribute to the growth your business aspires to.

I'm almost certain that you will have given due consideration to each of the key areas in turn, and you may already have begun to consider a number of options to address the issues you've identified. It's the eCommerce Foundations Roadmap in its entirety that elevates implementation.

CHAPTER 2

SECURITY AND MAINTENANCE

Every hour, every minute of every day sees websites around the globe being attacked with malicious intent. Not only that, but cybercrime continues to evolve at an alarming pace. The exploitation of the lack of secure networking opens up access pathways to robots/machines to scan sites for known vulnerabilities that can circumvent human attempts to prevent this. It's an endemic problem that every webshop CEO will be aware of and, no doubt, stringent efforts will be made to either prevent, or at least mitigate, against those risks.

Phishing is one of the more commonly used attack methods and is a type of social engineering. It refers to methods used by attackers to trick victims – typically via email, text, or phone – into providing private information, such as passwords, account numbers, social security numbers and any amount of identifiable information.

One such high profile incident occurred in September 2022 when the internal databases of Uber were compromised by an 18-year-old hacker. This individual gained access to Uber's secure data through 'social engineering'. This refers to methods used by similar attackers to trick victims – typically via email, text, or phone – into providing private information, such as passwords, account numbers, social security numbers and any amount of identifiable information. In this instance, the hacker (when arrested) blamed Uber's ineffective security measures in making the breach possible by posing as a corporate information technology worker. He is reported to have convinced an Uber contractor to reveal the password to its systems.

Such manipulation methods are becoming commonplace in the world of cybercrime, as are malware and ransomware which infect a website. Worryingly, most webshop owners typically won't notice. This is because attackers normally infect the webshop and install tools to allow them to further continue to exploit it in some way; for example, to send spam or insert spam links to fake merchant sites that cleverly impersonate the original, thus fooling consumers to part with their valuable financial information. Webshop owners are normally warned by their hosting companies after the malware has been detected and that results in it being taken down to prevent further damage.

Downtime is expensive for any webshop. Knowing and spotting security threats and defects can seem like an endless task, best left to the experts, although I am of the strong opinion that security should remain a top priority for every executive leadership team. As a consumer yourself, you'll rest easier at night knowing that at the very least your operation offers consumers SSL[5] certificate protection. At this level, nobody needs to be a security expert to understand the need for this basic level of protection.

Moreover, Google also checks that this measure is in place so that when customers search for your site, they can on further interrogation be notified with the message 'Your connection to this site is secure'.

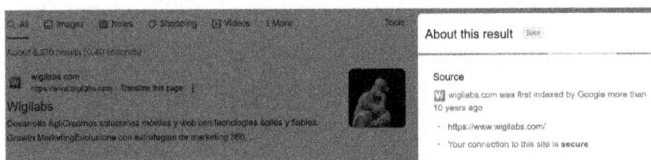

The question from your perspective is, how secure is your webshop operation? Websites that use WordPress as their CMS (Content Management System) are frequently targeted by hackers.

In fact, in 2019 94% of successful cyberattacks against CMS-powered websites targeted WordPress sites,[6] commanding as it does a 65.1% share of the CMS market (representing 43.2%[7] of all websites on the internet in 2022, up from 39.5% in 2021). However, because it's also an open platform, it's consistently checked for numerous parties and experts for ongoing and unplugged vulnerabilities. In that sense, WordPress has a distinct advantage as a result of its global community of willing and voluntary 'safeguarders' over a one-stop, ready-made eCommerce private company platform you could have chosen instead to host your webshop.

Third-party sites certainly offer the 'peace of mind' factor in that the buck stops with them. However, therein lies the problem when it comes to security – because as and when a security issue inevitably occurs, the client has no visibility in attempting to fix it and, as such, they are left powerless to act in their own interest. That security threat doesn't always stem from outside of the vendor themselves, as was the case in September 2021.

Shopify suffered a data breach at the hands of two of its third-party customer support team. They were persuaded by an individual seeking to gain a competitive advantage to steal customer details and transactional records. Although Shopify was named as the victim in the resultant court case, it could be argued that the 200 of its small business clients were the real victims of aggravated identity theft and conspiracy to commit wire fraud. None of this was their fault, but equally, they were powerless to act. Shopify has also been criticised for using particularly weak password policies that are at least five characters in length and that don't contain spaces at either end. Such passwords today can be breached almost instantly.

For some, the risk outweighs the advantages of using third parties to operate payment card gateways on their behalf, but it's a risk all the same. The reality of such an arrangement means that they're left at the mercy of the vendor. That's one of the key differences between third-party vendors and WordPress/WooCommerce.

With WordPress/WooCommerce you take on the responsibility and ownership of keeping your store safe, but you're backed by the thousands that are also in the same boat and not left hanging onto a customer support ticket. Nobody wants to play the inevitable ping-pong correspondence chain until the matter is addressed.

Perhaps that was one of your motivations when you selected WordPress or WooCommerce? Their multi-collaborative, open-source platforms offer the fast and flexible option to search for resolutions from amongst its worldwide collective community made up of thousands of similar users. No problem is absolutely unique and hasn't already been encountered, where a solution can't be tailored for your webshop's own use.

The huge advantage of WordPress and WooCommerce is that you benefit from all those hours that have been spent developing the platform already and the continual string of plugin updates based on user experiences that the larger platforms, such as Shopify etc., find difficult to compete with at speed; that, and including cost and commission fees. The more a webshop is successful, the more those costs will be.

Of course, for start-ups or small-scale operations, those costs and commissions are more bearable and those commercial platforms are ideal, but once a business begins to grow, those costs begin to impact the profit lines. Linking this back to security as an area of concern, the decision not to use a private platform to host your webshop is, therefore, key to the security decisions within your operation. If cost has been your primary motivation, then security needs to be your **number one priority**.

Therefore, this chapter takes a deep dive into those key areas in order to highlight where there may be vulnerabilities that may not be immediately obvious as risk factors. Being more aware of the fundamentals of this security pillar ensures that you:

- have the right foundations set up in order to handle your customers' data

- protect/defend your webshop's store from the myriad of attacks that go on 24/7 on the internet

- comply with Google's (and others) view of a secure webshop

- prevent ill-intentioned people from hijacking your webshop, making fake orders, accessing client or card processing information

- implement best practices for the people on your team: employees, partners, vendors and freelancers

- are proactive, not reactive, when an attack or security crisis has already occurred.

MAINTENANCE

When the aim is to grow the business, it's tempting to focus on increasing its marketing activity. Yes, that is important, but often it's at the expense of carrying out essential maintenance on the platform. It's not an 'either/or' option, but all too often the leadership team loses sight of security as an ongoing priority.

In reality, security is always in a state of flux. As criminal activity becomes more sophisticated, so do the preventative solutions developed, and the beauty of WordPress is that its collective community is continually developing plugins and updates to meet these new threats posed by external parties. There is no such thing as a one-time, one-size-fits-all security problem solver, because a security fix implemented one month ago may well be obsolete and ineffective the next. There is no room for complacency, because that's akin to leaving your windows and doors wide open to opportunist threats and risks of being attacked.

Managing and implementing updates in order to decrease that risk, therefore, needs to be as much part of the leadership DNA as does its marketing ambitions, not just for future development, but also in assessing retrospectively. In all probability, a typical webshop using WordPress or WooCommerce etc., will rely on the expertise of third party tech experts to take them from a standing start to winning the race. The bespoke nature of the business operation requires similarly bespoke code that's often not been tested or scanned properly for vulnerabilities, leaving it unsecure in a fast-moving digital landscape. In which case, that coding needs urgent review.

Think of security as if it were an onion comprising layer upon layer. The fact is, the more the business grows, the more it needs to add more layers to the onion. Problems arise, however, as those layers become over-looked or forgotten about as your third party experts move on and nobody really understands how to imple-ment them correctly. Maintaining records, knowledge sharing and best practice handovers as a priority helps plug those internal vulnerabilities in dealing with increasing levels of 'tech debt'.

TECH DEBT AND
MARIE KONDO

Tech debt[8] (also known as code debt) accumulates as the result of prioritising speedy delivery and taking shortcuts in developing code as a quick fix, short-term solution. At some point, however, this will require attention as some code becomes obsolete or fails to meet its goals over time.

There are two schools of thought on how to approach this. One is to carry out a 'spring clean', favoured by many CTOs. During this process everything grinds to a halt as focus is directed primarily on all resources needed to thoroughly clean and refactor the code. And then there's this, inspired by Marie Kondo, the best-sell-ing author of *The Life-Changing Magic of Tidying Up*[9]. Her philosophy, followed by thousands worldwide, promotes a regular tidy up as a path to happiness. Her inspirational book on the 6 Rules is equally applicable to tidying up code. That got me thinking – why not apply those same rules to tidying up technical debt? Kondo suggests:

1. Commit yourself to tidying up – do a little every day. Little by little. Don't give up. Take breaks if you need to.

2. Imagine your ideal lifestyle – write out what you want your life to be about. Take time to concentrate your thoughts on what matters most.

3. Finish discarding first – go through old things before sifting through the things you love.

4. Tidy by category, not by location – do things by category. Kondo breaks it down to clothing, books, paper, miscellaneous and sentimental items.

5. Follow the right order – don't veer off the course. You'll be tempted to go on to other categories while finishing one. Don't! Do your best to finish one by one.

6. Ask yourself if it sparks joy – after all unnecessary things are removed, pull out the essentials and ask, *'Does this produce joy?'*

I was impressed by the simplicity and logical thinking behind Kondo's *6 Rules of Tidying Up* because, as a process, it can be applied across the board, including Tech Debt. This rule book forces us to literally avoid creating a pile-high mess that we then have to somehow navigate ourselves out of. Tech Debt is handled best by not creating a mess; it's about de-junking as we go along, saving time and resources for where it's needed most. Like, now.

THIRD PARTY DEVELOPMENT PARTNERS

When an eCommerce business relies on working with third party co-operation partners to create, develop and achieve its goals, especially in the early days of start-up, this flags up some inherent risks, irrespective of any initial goodwill. In so doing, the business opens its doors to 'strangers' to whom it will grant access to its data, including, potentially, its clients.

Unfortunately, in rare instances this relationship can turn sour for any number of reasons, or at the very least, can risk their clients' data to future potential misuse. Therefore, it's essential any security gaps are plugged from the outset by creating development environments where partners only have the necessary access to its eCommerce platform **without** access to its client data. That means ring-fencing access to identifiable personal information, such as:

- customers' first and last names
- billing addresses
- financial information
- purchasing history.

This isn't as draconian or unnecessary as it might seem. For example, imagine that a high-profile celebrity engaged a firm to install security measures at their home address – the expectation would be that they would arrive, install the equipment, test it and leave without the need for access to the celebrity's private life. Their task is limited only to providing the essential protection without further interrogation. It's also highly likely that celebrity has vetted the vendor to the highest degree in order to feel secure in the knowledge that no hidden cameras will be installed to maliciously spy on them.

The same principle above should apply to every eCommerce business leader when engaging third party developers – they should undergo a similar and rigorous vetting process to ensure that their security will not be compromised, especially if that relationship were to end on bad terms. Without this check in place, the business potentially risks third parties exerting unnecessary leverage that can damage it.

For example, one of my clients had previously engaged remote freelancers to assist developing their webshop operation. When their working relationship deteriorated, however, the freelancers blocked access to the eCommerce shop. It was nothing short of commercial blackmail in that they demanded a payment to release the block they'd imposed.

Sadly, this is more common than widely known and yet it's avoidable by engaging well-known larger entities and issuing a water-tight contract of service (together with the expense that involves). Or, if a business decides to engage a smaller agency (or freelancers), then they should make a selection based on the results of necessary due diligence.

- Always begin any such relationship with the reassurance they are trustworthy.

- Check their testimonials and reviews first via sites such as Trustpilot.

- And **never** grant access to live data!

No reputable third party ever expects a business to provide that access. Any that does should raise a well-deserved red flag.

PASSWORDS

Strong passwords might seem to be the most obvious and basic requirement. I would agree were it not for the fact that passwords are not always as high on the tick list as they should be. Your own personal password may be cast iron in its capability to withstand an attack, but unfortunately, there are always others in the leadership team that rely on weak passwords, mainly because they're memorable. Naturally, as human beings we're flawed individuals and so we sometimes like to take the path of least resistance. In respect of password security, however, there's no room for such complacency.

For the avoidance of any doubt, a weak password is the easiest gateway for a hacker to successfully carry out a login attack. It's one of the most frequent means of infiltrating an online business through its front door. Everyone, the leadership team included, with back-office access to the business must ensure that their password is strong[10] and, furthermore, is enabled with two step, or multiple factor authentication.[11]

As a fundamental principle, only employ the strongest of passwords. This should be strict company policy that's universally adhered to. The following graphic shows why.

USING CHATGPT HARDWARE TO BRUTE FORCE YOUR PASSWORD IN 2023

Number of Characters	Numbers Only	Lowercase Letters	Upper and Lowercase Letters	Numbers, Upper and Lowercase Letters	Numbers, Upper and Lowercase Letters, Symbols
4	Instantly	Instantly	Instantly	Instantly	Instantly
5	Instantly	Instantly	Instantly	Instantly	Instantly
6	Instantly	Instantly	Instantly	Instantly	Instantly
7	Instantly	Instantly	Instantly	Instantly	Instantly
8	Instantly	Instantly	Instantly	Instantly	1 secs
9	Instantly	Instantly	4 secs	21 secs	1 mins
10	Instantly	Instantly	4 mins	22 mins	1 hours
11	Instantly	6 secs	3 hours	22 hours	4 days
12	Instantly	2 mins	7 days	2 months	8 months
13	Instantly	1 hours	12 months	10 years	47 years
14	Instantly	1 days	52 years	608 years	3k years
15	2 secs	4 weeks	2k years	37k years	232k years
16	15 secs	2 years	140k years	2m years	16m years
17	3 mins	56 years	7m years	144m years	1bn years
18	26 mins	1k years	378m years	8bn years	79bn years

HIVE SYSTEMS ⟩ Learn how we made this table at **hivesystems.io/password**

Password hacking timeline.
Image courtesy of Hive Systems, please visit the source webpage (https://www.hivesystems.io/password)

This graphic serves as a stark reminder that many attacks today target people and not just systems. It's of paramount importance to ensure that not only the business but also your customers are educated against phishing attacks and are offered tips on their own device protection. The main message for all is: be rigorous with password selections to avoid accounts from being attacked.

Additionally, tell your customers explicitly that your webshop will never ask them to confirm their password or credit card information. This hack attack alone accounts for up to 96% of consumer security violations. And, because as humans we're flawed, there are rare occasions when employees exploit those vulnerabilities at customers' expense. It's not a pleasant thought but it happens, and when it occurs it can create untold reputational damage.

The solution is to delineate access:

- Not everyone needs permissions to manage a universal admin account.
- Instead, create separate profiles into component areas with their own permission schemes.

Should there then be a security attack, it will only affect a specific profile without exposing the whole administration to danger. In limiting shared permissions, it's more difficult to expose the business to internal vulnerability.

AUDIT, AUDIT, AUDIT!

It's not always easy to keep abreast of everything security related, almost impossible for most businesses given the speed and levels of inventiveness that intruders operate at. To mitigate the risks, it's essential to seek support from professionals so that your IT team is acutely aware of all current threats to the business. However, engaging reputable cybersecurity expert firms to audit your entire webshop may prove difficult and expensive.

It's worth exploring available options provided by groups of independent security researchers that can audit your business (some for free on non-profit platforms such as openbugbounty.org). Start by creating an account and open a bug hunt for free. The security experts will then begin to analyse your site and proactively detect and report any problems they find.

I'd also recommend a service that automatically identifies issues through static code review analysis, such as codacy.com (especially if you employ in-house development teams). This service notifies businesses about security issues, code coverage, code duplication, and code complexities directly from its current workflow. It's also free to use and is available for open-source projects.

- Audit your webshop security frequently.

- Take advantage of the latest maintenance updates.

- Plug existing and new vulnerabilities.

- Install the latest security updates.

- Use a Web Application Firewall (WAF) like Cloudflare.

- Make sure every admin on your WooCommerce has two-factor authentication set up.

- Keep WordPress core and plugins updated. I recommend waiting no more than 7 days for an update. That is enough to prevent you from getting any undetected bugs from a new release while at the same time not falling behind on new security updates.

CASE STUDY: FORTIFYING AN ECOMMERCE STORE AGAINST CYBER THREATS

Overview

In this example, an online food retail company was using WooCommerce to power their eCommerce store and had outsourced much of its technical and software operations to freelancers. Engaging third parties is not the core issue. Indeed, such arrangements can bring a wealth of positive attributes to any business (as I will describe later, as long as the relationship is securely ring fenced). However, the unforced error the webshop made here was that it granted freelancers access to its client data.

Best practice would have meant that freelancers **only** had access to the webshop's **source code**. Therefore, when one particular rogue freelancer then blocked the webshop's access to its valuable client data, the retailer faced multiple security challenges, including data breaches and customer information theft. As a result, I was contacted to help them to take proactive steps to enhance their store's future security.

Actions Taken

1. Regular vulnerability scans and penetration tests conducted to identify potential weaknesses in their system.

2. Two-factor authentication (2FA) implemented for admin access, with additional strengthened password policies.

3. A schedule that regularly updated WooCommerce and all plugins was introduced to ensure the latest security patches were installed.

4. Malicious activities, such as brute-force attacks and suspicious login attempts, were monitored and blocked utilising a reputable security plugin.

Outcomes

By implementing these essential security measures, this retailer significantly reduced the risk of security breaches. They experienced no further data breaches or incidents of customer information theft. This increased their customers' confidence in shopping on their website, leading to higher sales and improved brand reputation.

SUMMARY

Like it or not, security is your **number one priority**. From it, every other single part of the business flows. Security is the foundation stone. If the business isn't built upon security, then at some point (sooner, not later) it will crumble.

In many ways, it's a cat and mouse game with malicious perpetrators leaving most of us continually running to catch up. However, it's your job to ensure you're as far ahead as possible so that your business remains protected. Security may not always be top of the agenda when starting an eCommerce business, when the initial aim is to get the first clients through the door, but you must invest the necessary time and resources into security from Day 1. Avoid the common mistake of trying to play catch up in fixing it. Otherwise, it will only cost the business dearly both in money and reputational damage when things go wrong.

Ensure that security maintenance is built into your normal business cycle as mandatory and that your security policies and protocols are your proactive first priority above all else. I strongly advise you to make essential your commitment to security housekeeping and insist that maintenance contracts are in place where your internal team never lose sight of them.

WordPress and similar platforms might be free to use, but that doesn't free the business of its responsibilities to itself and its customer base. Security is the bedrock on which your business will thrive, so it must be both extensive and **thorough**. It's you that can lead those conversations and be on the same page as your IT experts. Share that responsibility in being the guardian of the business's data. That data is worth securing and protecting at all costs.

- Maintain and update all WordPress core/plugins/themes.

- Verify your third party development partners' credentials and reputation.

- Insist on strong passwords internally and educate your customers.

- Work with professionals and have an ongoing maintenance contract.

CHAPTER 3

PERFORMANCE

WooCommerce has become synonymous with flexibility and scalability. However, the level of customisation and flexibility can often lead to subpar performance, especially if your store is not optimised correctly. Poor site performance not only tarnishes the user experience but can also negatively impact search engine rankings and, consequently, revenue. Thus, WooCommerce performance optimisation is not just an option; it's a necessity.

This chapter aims to serve as a guide to understanding, diagnosing, and resolving performance issues within your WooCommerce environment. We delve into the nuances of server requirements, database optimisations, front-end speed, and various caching mechanisms. Whether you're a novice store owner bewildered by sluggish loading times or a seasoned developer looking to scale, the strategies outlined here are designed to offer tangible improvements in performance metrics.

The key takeaway? Time is money – quite literally so in the world of eCommerce. A delay of even one second in page load time can result in significant revenue loss and decreased customer satisfaction. Therefore, optimising your WooCommerce store's performance isn't just technical housekeeping; it's a critical business activity that has a direct impact on your bottom line.

So, buckle up and prepare to turbocharge your WooCommerce store; a high-speed, smooth-sailing online shopping experience awaits your customers.

Without optimised performance, and in particular with mobile, the risks this presents are:

- Slow growth due to the fact it limits sales and deters visitors from browsing. In technical terms we call this a 'bottleneck'. That's like a super busy supermarket only having one checkout counter where frustrated lines of customers abandon their shopping carts, perhaps never to return.

- Losing revenue and customers to competitors due to a webshop's technical errors, or worse, outages.

Neither of the above is a good prospect for the enter-prising CEO and their leadership team. That explains why so often they rely on the tech experts to prevent, or fix, these bottleneck issues. That's completely under-standable, since the area of performance optimisation is littered with technical jargon and solutions best left to the IT experts.

I partly agree that performance optimisation is not simply a technical issue. It's also a strategic mindset and ongoing concern that everybody in the executive team needs to embrace. The truth is that it's also hard to get right and all too often I've seen teams make the following common mistakes where they:

1. Ignore it.
2. Wing it.
3. Under-invest in extra future capacity.
4. Firefight, instead of fire prevention.

Also, depending on your independent provider, there are a number of variables that also throw a spanner into the works. For example, WooCommerce isn't ide-ally optimised for speed and growth whilst WordPress pretty much leaves you to your own devices. Much will depend on how well the webshop has been designed and built. This flexibility is the principal reason so many webshop owners choose WordPress and WooCommerce. The fact that there is no one set of rules or protocols to follow as opposed to the costly fixed parameter solutions provided by the bigger commercial hosts. That might also explain, however, why many webshops lack the understanding to help them achieve optimised growth.

Performance is ultimately about speed and how that impacts on the user experience. Unfortunately, I've often seen how poor speed is a contributory factor to a client's slow growth. Customer expectations have been raised by the likes of Google, Amazon, Uber, Netflix and Airbnb etc. Faster speed leads to better results. In that respect, Amazon sets the benchmark, having discovered that when returned results speeds were reduced by one second, then conversions increased. Amazon also famously learned that every 100ms of latency cost them 1% in sales. For any modern online business, performance equates to company performance. Therefore, the reputational and financial consequences of less-than-excellent load times can be brutal.

According to Aberdeen Research, three seconds appears to be the breakpoint for all web users. Compared to a one-second load time, abandonment rates triple. Any more than three seconds, 20% of visitors abandon the site and move on to a better-performing competitor instead.

Kissmetrics discovered even more dramatic numbers. According to their figures, 40% of consumers abandon a webshop if it takes more than three seconds to load. But that's not all: Kissmetrics also found that just a one-second delay in page response can result in a 7% reduction in conversions. For a webshop generating $100,000 per day, this percentage translates to $2.5 million in lost sales per year. That's a pretty expensive one second.

More importantly for independent webshop owners is the fact that Google also uses performance as a metric to rank sites more highly than others depending on load speed. This is part of their drive to raise the bar in the market via their Core Web Vitals analytics. The better a webshop's core vitals, the more Google's search algorithms will favour it. Performance, therefore, has risen up executive leaders' attention scale. That doesn't imply it's simple to deal with. In fact, because it's an area rooted in technical jargon, many CEOs are happier delegating it to their IT teams, or, worse still, ignoring it completely as opposed to making an effort to understand the underlying principles. To their credit, most recognise that where Google sets the standard, something must be done about their own site's performance in order to maximise growth. Nobody wants to languish at the foot of Google's rankings.

What's the key learning here? As a general rule, between one to three seconds is where you need to be in terms of acceptable load times. Anything under one second where a page load feels almost instant is the Holy Grail. Anything over five seconds results in lower conversion rates (sales, enquiries, phone calls, bookings and so forth) because it doesn't compare favourably to competitors. However, be aware not all webshops can achieve this as third-party code, such as Facebook Pixels, Livechat and other marketing tools usually slow them down.

It's clear that Google is aligned with the consumers' mindset; any page/result that takes 'too long' to load diminishes the window of opportunity to retain the consumer's attention. Instead, they will be lost to one of many likely simultaneous distractions or notifications. It's all too easy for people to click away from a sales page onto a news bulletin elsewhere and to abandon a shopping cart.

Part of the performance solution is to tackle it as early as possible. However, many start-ups will focus too much of their initial efforts on sales and marketing strategies by utilising an existing theme or plugin on a minimum viable platform. After what may seem like a good start, they usually soon find themselves treading water because the performance is below par (even more apparent since Google implemented its core web vital metrics in 2021).

Even those that are at a more advanced growth stage can equally be negatively affected by poor performance metrics. To counter this, they fall into the same old trap when they create ever increasingly attractive marketing campaigns to persuade more customers through their 'doors' whilst still having a 'one checkout' mindset. However, they soon realise that it's their webshop's poor performance that leads to poor sales. Add to this, users inevitably experience substandard front-end service, such as the wrong item dispatched, a refund query, the need to return goods, etc.

WooCommerce is especially known for its slow admin/back office due to large volumes of orders, and so it's essential that a webshop's back office also performs efficiently and at speed. Customers don't like to be kept waiting whilst an operative attempts to locate their details, or order. The longer these processes take, the bigger the servicing cost. Those costs also grow when customer enquiry volumes increase exponentially as the business grows. Therefore, the managing and exporting huge volumes of business data analytics/insights also need to be optimised. The longer this takes, the greater the expense in terms of both actual money, but also in time.

These performance problems call for a range of different performance optimisation solutions since there are no specific 'out of the box' options available for the WordPress or WooCommerce user. The decisions made will affect the entire business, even the brand, because their impact extends way beyond the nuts and bolts of the operation.

It takes a team effort to resolve these issues, and that includes the leadership. It's also a reflection of the executives' strategic forward direction of travel and how they want the business to be perceived by customers in a crowded marketplace. Performance optimisation will always be an ongoing issue that needs to be constantly monitored by all. This can be especially difficult if there's no single person assigned to that role within the business (which is often the case).

A good place to start is to access where you are in terms of performance. Poorly performing metrics will feel painful, but the next response should be to assign someone to permanently manage and monitor performance, both public facing and back office operations. Doing so will greatly improve the reputation of the user experience, from sales to solving customer problems. The better optimised these processes, the more likely customers will return and recommend to others.

Performance is not simply a customer issue, it impacts on every business process that interacts with the platform. It requires total logistical integration, from point of sale, supply chain all the way through to the last mile delivery partner. This represents innovative strategic team thinking at its best.

You only need to look at Amazon to see its remarkable operation in action, driven by optimised performance. Every independent can – and should – adopt a similar mindset. It requires a proactive bigger picture approach, not a *reactive* one. It's about anticipating what will be the worst case scenario and committing the necessary resources to prevent this, so that you can enjoy the fruits of success. Mindset is all.

My experience has shown me that there are two types of CEOs:

1. Very aggressively growth orientated and eager to get the ball rolling as soon as possible. Feels stuck once the initial growth curve plateaus out. They then need to find solutions to fix the inevitable crisis that follows.

2. More focused on actual performance. From the outset they are mindful of the requirements in order for the whole product offering to be right, from start to finish.

You can probably guess which of the two types of CEO I admire most. I am convinced, through evidence-based results, that it makes sense to prioritise Performance because it's a fundamental factor in contributing to growth. Even if your business is already considering a redesign of its webshop, I'd urge you to build in performance requirements as a central tenet. Or, if you're opening in a new market, the same applies.

It's no different to creating the fastest train on Earth. If the wrong tracks are laid down, that train will not perform at its best. No matter how sleek, luxurious or fast it could go, it will always run into performance problems, leaving the customer dissatisfied. Quite possibly, in your own operation, you may not even be aware that even the smallest performance impediment exists. In all probability, that could be the one thing that slows down your webshop's growth because Performance has not been prioritised from day one.

In short, both the Executive and IT teams need to be aligned. They must agree upon the webshop's performance standard that then matches their aspirations for growth. This is surprisingly lacking in many small businesses with ambitions. Often the leaders will believe that style over substance will do the trick; they create eye-catching graphics and layouts to showcase special offers using attractors and sizzle. For pure marketing purposes, of course, this is necessary, but if the webshop's performance sucks, then the sizzle will fizzle.

WARNING! It's not just customers that will notice and remember poor performance; remember, Google monitors and reports performance invisibly in the background. If you're not worried by this, then you should be. Google now officially factors its PageSpeed[12] scores into SEO rankings for online stores, so it would be a wise move to get ahead of this now otherwise a poor ranking will see your traffic fall away.

A top tip: successful WooCommerce webshops rely heavily on organic traffic as a result of expertly worded SEO terms that Google returns in search enquiries. This reduces their advertising spend and reliance on paid for traffic via AdWords or Facebook ads. Hence, performance is a super critical area to address. In the eCommerce world, any ranking improvement that sees Google elevate yours from 'poor' speed to 'good' can literally close the gap between financially poor to rich, as reflected in upticks in revenue, conversions and rankings!

Management guru Peter Drucker says it best: 'If you can't measure it, you can't improve it.' To know whether or not your webshop is high performing you must, therefore, continuously track performance.

HPOS (HIGH-PERFORMANCE ORDER STORAGE)

High-Performance Order Storage (HPOS) is a Woo-Commerce feature designed using custom database tables. It shows great promise for shaping the future of WooCommerce in that its specific function is to optimise order data storage and retrieval for eCommerce needs (instead of relying on the posts and postmeta tables by default). It minimises the impact on the store's performance as it grows while, at the same time, enabling efficient handling of large volumes of orders.

Its main benefit is that it empowers businesses of all sizes to effortlessly scale their operations without the need for extensive technical expertise or interventions. Prior to its introduction, large WooCommerce stores required extensive technical expertise which could represent a strain on much needed resources. Where initially HPOS was made available to all stores as an opt-in feature in WooCommerce 7.1, going forward it will be enabled by default. As a result, my belief is that HPOS will play an increasingly pivotal role in shaping the future trajectory of WooCommerce.

"THE NORMAL PERFORMANCE CULPRITS"

In respect of poor performance in WooCommerce, I regularly see the following common culprits:

- **Hosting** – inadequate hosting services, such as shared hosting with limited resources or unreli-able servers. This can lead to slow loading times and overall sluggish performance.

- **Non-optimised database** – as the WooCom-merce store grows and accumulates a significant amount of data, it's essential to optimise the database regularly to ensure efficient querying and retrieval of information.

- **Multilingual plugins** – whilst employing these can be beneficial for expanding the reach of an online store, they can (and do) sometimes affect performance. These plugins often introduce additional processing and translation overhead, which can impact page load times and responsiveness.

- **Custom plugins** – any that are poorly coded or not optimised can also drag down performance. Inefficient code, excessive database queries, or compatibility issues with other plugins can lead to slowdowns and performance issues.

- **Poorly coded themes** – bloated themes with excessive design elements, unnecessary scripts, or poorly optimised code can result in longer loading times and decreased overall performance.

It's important to note that the default versions of WordPress/WooCommerce are quite fast. However, when additional plugins and customisations are added on top, they can potentially degrade performance. When faced with such performance issues, troubleshoot the affected issues by removing plugins or customisations and assess their negative impacts on performance. By gradually eliminating potential culprits, it becomes easier to pinpoint and address the specific elements that drag down performance and, as a result, optimise your WooCommerce store accordingly.

For an example of a WooCommerce shop that is highly optimised, please visit the Telldus website at **https://telldus.com/**

CASE STUDY: WEB PERFORMANCE

Overview

An online clothing store powered by WooCommerce noticed its slow page load times resulted in high bounce rates and decreased conversions. The problem was that, despite the fact the webshop's design was fresh and engaging, as its traffic steadily increased from a low base, its original prototype design was unable to handle additional capacity. When I was asked to evaluate the problems, it became clear that although it operated well enough, it wasn't optimised enough, hence the slow page loads (which impacted on the delightful UX that I describe in more detail in the following chapter). The reality was that the business hadn't thought far enough ahead in anticipation of the increased numbers of customers entering the site at any one time. Just like if you intend to operate a slow train service, the tracks don't need to be as high spec as a high-speed service. The bullet train would soon come off its rails on a regional line, which is why it runs on tracks that are optimised to allow the service provider to operate on a completely different level altogether. The same principle applies to websites that anticipate high volumes of traffic.

This is especially important when it comes to page load times following a high-profile marketing campaign. Anything that slows the customer down risks them abandoning their pursuit of happiness. Therefore, the challenge for this client was to improve its website's performance, to enhance the user experience and thus increase customer retention.

Actions taken

1. Compressed and optimised images to reduce file sizes without compromising quality.

2. Leveraged caching mechanisms, such as browser caching and server-side caching, to store and serve frequently accessed content more efficiently.

3. Utilised a content delivery network (CDN) to distribute their website's static content across multiple servers worldwide.

4. Implemented lazy loading for images and implemented asynchronous loading for non-critical scripts to prioritise the display of visible content.

Outcomes

After implementing these web performance optimisations, the company observed significant improvements in their website's speed. Page load times decreased by 40%, resulting in a 25% decrease in bounce rates and a 15% increase in conversions. Customers were more satisfied with the faster and more responsive website, leading to increased sales and improved user retention.

SUMMARY

Invest in performance and make it a priority!

Raise your awareness about your webshop's performance. This isn't simply the sole responsibility of the technical team. It requires a collectively aligned vision from the beginning that matches future plans for growth. Performance is an accelerator that leads to growth.

Ideally, your eCommerce webshop will load in under one second in every territory that your target market resides in. That's the magical number that feels instant.

Help is always at hand, even if that means turning to external partners.

- Test with Google and until Google says you're ok, you're not ok.
- Until your Core Web Vitals are green, keep iterating.
- Keep improving.

A final word of reassurance is that performance issues are not a unique experience to any one business. They've each had their emergency call-out moments either internally, or to external partners, to help resolve unexpected problems. However, once resolved and performance is optimised, your webshop could be known as one of the fastest in the market.

As a result, it will set a gold standard that others will want to emulate. In recognition of that, not only will your performance be celebrated, so will your leadership skills in embracing performance as a pinnacle within the eCommerce landscape.

CHAPTER 4

CREATE A DELIGHTFUL USER EXPERIENCE

"People love delightful digital experiences. It can make the dullest of tasks an exciting experience, like filling in forms and paying for groceries. So why aren't all digital experiences delightful?"

**MARTIN SKARBØ SANGOLT,
IN THE IMPORTANCE OF DELIGHTFUL UX[13]**

This quote resonates with me on so many levels. At its heart, it suggests that even the most mundane of online purchases should be the result of an equally delightful user experience as purchasing a luxury item. It's not simply the product that drives the sale, it's how the experience connects to the user. A delightful UX is more likely to result in goods in the shopping cart. However, it's easy to fall out of sync with your customers if they experience problems using your webshop that haven't been spotted or occurred to you.

In this chapter, I encourage a rigorous approach in gaining a deeper understanding of real users' problems so that you can discover how best to solve them. That includes regularly engaging in meaningful conversations through which you not only learn about your clients, but also foster better relationships with them. This will significantly contribute towards providing a great service that ensures every user enjoys a delightful UX.

However, to achieve this there's no easy or fast-track option. This will be an ongoing, organic process that needs you driving this initiative at its heart. Your aim is to create a delightful UX that lets your customers create a genuine emotional connection with you. Too many webshops fall short of providing a delightful UX, which I believe is the single biggest reason that turns customers away. The priority has to be focused on delivering quality of service, not quantity of visitors. You'll know 'you got there' when your clients offer you feedback about the delightful UX they experienced.

Therefore, avoid the temptation to prioritise increasing traffic to the webshop before gaining mastery of both usability and delivering. Take it one step at a time. Often, I will encourage my clients to invest 4-6 weeks on this step alone in order to ensure substantial progress. The good news is that, once this step is mastered, clients tend to see rapid progress during the first week of roll out. But in all honesty, this timeline will vary from business to business and yours is no exception. It may take longer but it is still a worthwhile investment. This step is a vital element of your strategic growth plan that elevates your brand from average to premium as a result of effort to go above and beyond what your competitors offer. The goal is for your brand to be seen as remarkable as you look to grow and scale the business into new markets.

Your future success relies on your customers' journey, from the first step of finding your webshop online, browsing your products to then making a purchase. That entire process needs to be fast, smooth and feel intuitive.

Despite your best efforts to date to achieve this, the results tell a different story. Do you still need to know what took customers away from the checkout and took their money off the table? This is a common question

I'm often asked by webshop owners who feel they've done everything right in laying down the foundations.

The short answer is, it's mainly a lack of connection between you and the customer, no matter how much your site looks like Amazon. And by the way, when I say 'you' I really do mean it's *you* and your leadership team.

However, let me reassure you that this is easily fixed by following the three steps below that will deepen the connection between you, your webshop and your customers. This requires some reverse engineering and for you to 'roll up your sleeves and get your hands dirty', but believe me when I say that this will be a rewarding effort.

Going that 'extra mile' means changing your mindset: it's not simply thinking about the site in functional terms, but also thinking about it in emotional terms. That's because behind every search enquiry and transaction is a real person. Of course, none of us can second guess a customer's mindset when arriving at a webshop, and in reality, they can stumble upon yours for any variety of reasons. What you **can** do, however, is better understand the fact that even users may not be aware they have a need for what it is you offer until they see it. On that basis you should be mindful of the fact they fall into one of the following three categories:

1. THE BUSY BROWSER

Like it or not, busy people have no immediate need for your products or services even if they know that at some point in the future they might. They are more likely to be:

- preoccupied with more important issues that don't include making an immediate purchase or enquiry

- unfocused, although they may possibly return when their need becomes more front of mind

- stubborn in their refusal to engage, no matter how hard you try to entice them, they simply tell you they don't need it just yet.

The best you can hope for is that they might open an email, but they're just too busy to take your offer any further. You could choose to continue to court their interest over time through informative and interesting marketing mail shots. Possibly at some unidentifiable point in the future they might eventually convert into a sale, but this will be very much in their own time when they're able to afford the time.

2. THE PROBLEM SEEKER

You might think a customer with a pressing problem to solve would be the ideal, easy catch if your solution is the perfect match. The problem is, when they arrive at your webshop for the first time, they'll take a lot of convincing that you are, in fact, the answer to their prayers.

- They'll need more than a great offer to persuade them.

- They need to feel that you completely understand them and their needs.

- Your marketing content needs to resonate with and relate to them.

My advice is to:

- walk in their footsteps

- speak their language right from the beginning of your interactions

- describe how your experience reflects their own and how your solution meets their need

- prove your authority and credentials in solving their problem through testimonials and case studies

- follow this with an irresistible call to action.

3. UNDECIDED

Similar to the customer above, they:

- know they have a problem

- have carried out their research on which solutions potentially work the best

- only remain half convinced your solution will provide the answers.

The problem is:

- they can't yet decide which of your options to choose

- they hesitate to commit, either because they're overwhelmed by choice (including from a competitor's site)

- they might reconsider the urgency to act straightaway.

Your challenge is to clearly delineate yours from any rival offer so that it stands out. It needs to reassure them that, if they buy from you, they're in safe hands and that doing nothing may only serve to prolong their problem. Finally, make them aware that, if they delay any further, they might miss out on the product availability or offer altogether. Help them decide to wait no longer and to buy now.

For me, empathy is the core foundation of all good marketing. When you treat customers with respect, trust follows. Studies reveal that behind every product or service lies a user's emotional needs that they're hoping to fulfil as a result. Once you have clarity on what their experience of your webshop is, then you can tailor the site and its marketing to reflect that in more impactful ways. The only way you can understand how your site connects is by stepping out of your own shoes into those of your customers.

To not ask these fundamental questions would be a mistake. The temptation is for a webshop team to look at its creation like a parent does at its baby – obviously they believe theirs is the most adorable child ever to be born. However, beauty is often in the eye of the beholder, and a subjective opinion is not always the best arbiter. Remember, your customers' reactions to their experience matter the most, even if at times that critique stings.

Whilst many of my clients identify areas of their webshop they want to improve, most changes prove to be cosmetic. The solution is to inspect data pathways that reveal **in real time** how customers navigate and interact with various components on the site. The good news is that this data almost certainly already sits within the business. The bad news is that it's rarely deployed, but once inspected, it becomes almost immediately apparent to identify where users experience those frustrating blockages. These can then be fixed, or removed, as a way of preventing users exiting the 'premises' (a solution not available to the bricks and mortar retailer).

Knowing how to turn that data into actionable insights adds value to the business and is good for customers, too, by enhancing the UX. It goes without saying that a delightful UX encourages users to leave positive referrals for other customers to follow their lead and visit the webshop. A knee-jerk response would be to immediately engage a third-party branding agent whose expertise will jazz up your webshop, perhaps to create a similar feel that echoes some of the successful, bigger brands in the marketplace.

There is some merit in leveraging that sense of familiarity; an increasing trend for many major online brands (such as Airbnb, Netflix or Uber etc.) is to mirror similar fonts, colours and themes that make users feel immediately comfortable. But hang on for a moment and pause before making that call. Remember, your brand extends way beyond how your site looks.

For customers, it's not just the familiarity of its visual layout and logo that matter, **it's the delightful UX that counts** because it's deeply entwined with the branding. For example, Netflix, users can scroll product selection horizontally, therefore when other brands emulate this, it suggests that the UX will be comparable. It's not just about looks, it's about how it **feels**.

Ideally, your webshop is driven by innovation and not limited by what already exists elsewhere online. Therefore, take time to discover what creates that delightful UX.

The good news again is that you're not yet a Netflix/Uber/Amazon. Being a small or medium business allows you to leverage your size in ways that the giants have simply lost touch with. They naturally have the advantage of resources and expensive infrastructure to manage custom at huge scale. On the flip side, their very size ensures that they lack the ability to truly connect with their customers (no matter how much their marketing messages say otherwise).

Start-ups and SMEs, on the other hand, have greater flexibility and more opportunities to build intimacy with which to leverage customer expectations. Their secret weapon is the ability to see for themselves how customers interact with their webshops as a result of real time analytics generated in granular detail on an ongoing process.

Be aware that a branding agency won't always tailor its package to include that level of detail, whereas you are already ideally placed to peel back the layers. Businesses like yours can more readily analyse data and learn where its brand aligns with both products and services in order to create a delightful UX.

Identifying users' emotional needs and the problems they wish to solve is a game changer. For example, selling cosmetics is more than simply populating a store filled with images of make-up. Typically, the customer's need is to want to look their best. This then makes them feel confident and it's that need to feel confident that initially drives their search. Landing on a product image, followed by a link to a shopping cart, won't fully achieve that. However, the ability to scroll through images of people just like them featured in familiar social situations using that product, will. That's because the journey depicted relates directly to the experience the customer seeks.

That contrasts directly to one of the most common webshop mistakes I see where a traditionally developed website remains almost entirely product image focused that lacks any empathy or connection to the UX (which is **not** delightful). These storefronts may announce they are the best in the world, but in fact they are purely utilitarian. Typically, they present grid offerings alongside functional copy about the product. It's a disappointingly clinical approach to sales, it feels remote and totally disconnected from the people they target, and lacks any relatable context of how the product will be used.

The UX deserves more than this if it's to drive growth in the business. Instead, it requires an intricate knowledge of the business sphere it operates within as well as a deeper connection with customers. Of course, efficient functionality is also essential as long as the UX is more than simply superficial.

I cannot emphasise enough how important it is to get to the heart of the customer's 'why?'. To ignore that deeper connection risks sending a subliminal message that your webshop doesn't actually care enough about their needs. The webshop might carry a superb range of products, it may even deliver reasonable results, but if it can't be bothered to go the extra mile, then why should its customers? Especially if a competitor within the same niche is already beginning to stand out in their eyes? When a customer leaves money on the table, you can be sure that the more connected competitor will pick it up.

AIM BEYOND 'SATISFACTION'

Many webshop business owners feel perplexed when their businesses fail to grow as they plateau and stagnate. I've seen many CEOs and Marketing Directors happy with their surveys and feedback forms telling them that their customers are 'satisfied'.

However, the reality is, there's a big distinction between a 'satisfactory' and a 'delightful' user experience. Customers automatically expect they will be 'satisfied' and assuming that expectation is met, you might think all is well and good. Yet this hides a much more worrying response. 'Satisfaction' may sound like a positive rating, but in fact it's neutral and it's more linked to a sense of **indifference** as research indicates.[14] That may come as a surprise, but when a customer's expectation is only superficially met, that says they were neither 'dissatisfied' nor 'overly surprised'.

I'm convinced that any CEO with ambitions to grow and scale their business would rather be aiming for the 'delightful' UX rather than 'satisfied'. In which case, their webshop not only needs to match expectation, it also needs to **exceed** it by introducing those elements that prompt the response '**delightful**', which differentiates it in remarkable ways compared to its more average-performing competitors.

Positively perceived differentiation helps drives growth acceleration and potentially becoming a premium brand. You'll know you've reached that point when your clients themselves tell you they're having a delightful experience and also because your webshop doesn't suffer continual churn.

With that in mind, I recommend the following steps to guide you in creating the pathway that builds towards the delightful UX experience:

STEP 1: GAIN A DEEPER UNDERSTANDING TO SOLVE REAL USER PROBLEMS

Every webshop has usability issues. A usability issue is anything that leads a user to an undesirable outcome. However, whilst these are relatively easy to spot, it's more difficult to know how to resolve them, if at all.

Creating a fully usable webshop begins by understanding what causes those issues. This in turn informs the measures required to help fix them. But please note, this isn't the moment to delegate this task to the IT and website designer teams. This must be a shared endeavour where the leadership team not only sets the agenda, but also remains in as much of the loop as everybody else. You personally won't necessarily know – or be expected to know – all the solutions.

You're not alone. Elon Musk wouldn't claim to be an engineer, but he was as much invested in developing automated car manufacturing lines for Tesla as he was being the visionary entrepreneur. He recognised that he also needed to be aware of any production line issues as much as his technical team. He even famously slept on the factory floor to show everyone that he was just as involved and not simply generating ideas in his 'ivory tower'. It was important for Musk to be by their side, to uncover problem areas and then work along-side his team to solve them. From a small business point of view, that ethic is equally as applicable: most webshop owners will know much of the business inside out, even if they personally don't have the expertise to implement improvement.

However, in my experience, more often than not, I've seen leadership teams farm out problem fixing to the 'experts'. There's little or no attempt to fully engage with the nuts and bolts. I advocate the opposite approach on the grounds that delegation cannot be **an abdication of responsibility**.

In a close-knit business it's essential everyone pulls together in the same direction to help the business to grow and scale. Even where there's a need to call in the experts, everyone must all work together. The leader-ship's knowledge of the business is vital in realising the vision of the bigger picture, married with the experts' understanding of where and why problems arise. Being stationed at ground zero is as important as being sur-rounded by the team of people to then create the delightful UX solutions.

The starting point is never as difficult as first imagined. When users experience problems – be that with pricing, information or products – they will tell you. Therefore, your Customer Support lead should also be a key member of the team that helps shape the delightful UX strategy. After all, their team sits at the frontline of the operation dealing with customer issues that arise from the back end of the business. Customer Support involvement is, therefore, equally as important in developing the delightful UX experience as the IT experts or creative and branding teams.

It's a collective effort across all points that the customer interacts with that demand a more forensic and detailed examination of what contributes (or doesn't) to that delightful UX. That includes every single visible and usable aspect of the site, from poorly worded content to functionality. A fantastically designed logo and brilliant looking site aren't the only solutions since they're cosmetic and don't scratch beneath the surface.

Therefore, when either your customers, frontline team or your trusted friends point you towards a problematic area:

- Listen to them.
- Take their feedback seriously.
- Work together.

- Pull the problem apart.

- Be honest.

- Acknowledge that the UX could be improved.

This multi-dimensional effort offers a variety of opinions and different options that may resolve many issues. If left to one team only, it will lack a 360 perspective. This is where you have the advantage on the grounds that your operation is not (yet) on the scale of Amazon; it's then perfectly placed to bring together all the relevant team members in one place to identify issues and meet challenges head on.

Your leadership input is, therefore, continually vital. Why? Because a delightful UX also sits at the heart of your ability to grow and scale your vision for the business. Of course, most leaders like you will always face 101 demands at any one time. They'd probably prefer to avoid yet another pressing concern. However, paying close attention to developing the delightful UX needs to be a top priority. If, like Elon Musk, you can roll up your sleeves and join your front-line colleagues, you'll soon leverage the valuable real-time data insights gained from closely inspecting your customer behaviour and feedback. This collective effort highlights any previously invisible or overlooked issues, especially since users' online behaviour is mostly unpredictable.

Any insights you will gain, therefore, add to the clarity as to where users experience difficulty and resulting signs of confusion need to be addressed. A picture will soon emerge that quickly tells you:

- Is your store a pleasure to use?

- Do your clients leave positive feedback about their experience within your store?

- Is your store efficient (easy to use, intuitive, fast)?

- Is your store effective (in generating sales and business results)?

- Do your clients understand everything on the webshop and on the navigation menus, without even having to click through?

STEP 2: INTUITIVE ACTION, NOT GUESSWORK

During a webshop's launch, it's impossible to anticipate where users will become stuck. That doesn't mean we shouldn't be looking out for them. WordPress offers a variety of compatible, high-performing software solutions, such as Hotjar and Crazyegg, that enable webshops to follow users' journeys from the moment they land and how often they:

- interact with the product page

- click

- scroll up and down.

It's an accepted fact that where a landing page's information or navigation isn't clear, customers tend to abandon the site almost immediately. If they do happen to continue to other pages, you can then carry out a full analysis of their behaviour in remarkable detail by tracking:

- cursor movements

- page views

- length of visit.

The bounce rate is a web analytics metric that quantifies the percentage of visitors who view a single page on a webshop and then leave without further interaction. The average eCommerce bounce rate is between 20% and 45%, anything lower than 20% is regarded as exceptional.[15]

What could be driving visitors away? Apart from slow-loading pages, usability issues are usually one of the most common factors. If users are unable to progress without experiencing problems, a high bounce is almost inevitable. Unfortunately, many webshops never know what that journey is like for their users.

One solution is 'heat mapping'. This visualisation of their journey is a simple means of pinpointing areas where a webshop needs to improve. Most importantly, this analysis identifies exactly where and when customers abandon the conversion funnel and leave. If their actions still remain unclear, it's possible to continue to interrogate by placing an on-page pop-up survey (following a 30-40 second delay) that asks what information they're still looking for[16] that enables you to:

- see the world through their eyes
- learn how to improve their experience
- identify any invisible bottlenecks.

Additionally, Google Optimise allows testing – and re-testing – of where navigation buttons perform best. Eventually it's possible to better understand users' behaviour patterns based on the insights gained as a result of variant testing. This then enables guiding them through their journey onwards towards conversion.

In the first instance, tell the tool to offer over a defined duration one version of your page to 50% of your audience, and a second version to the other 50%. At the end of the trial the analysis will inform which version performed the better.

Repeat the exercise as test 2, using the more successful version from test 1 pitted against a new variant, and monitor in similarly. Over time, confidence in the page's performance increases based on the data insights generated by customers' behaviour. It is they that will drive the webshop towards a more delightful UX.

Variant testing is the same principle that all the tech giants follow every day by way of creating small, iterative tests that lead to a fast, optimised UX. Invest in this process from the outset to provide you with an enviable, deeper knowledge of who your customers are. More importantly, you'll also understand first-hand the triggers that customers positively interact with.

STEP 3: INCREASE THE EMOTIONAL CONNECTIONS

Many business owners, after launching their webshop, are primarily focused on how to drive more visitors towards it with the intent of generating more sales. This is where my practice differs – as you will have already noticed, I won't delve into the area of conversions until later in the Foundations Roadmap as it's not the number one priority, as important as it is to address.

Steps 1 and 2 above are the precursors to creating that emotional connection between your webshop and your customer.

What exactly does that mean?

Imagine a webshop selling nothing but car component parts. These are hardly aspirational items in the traditional sense, and so you might reasonably wonder what an emotional connection has got to do with it. Compared to lifestyle goods that really do make customers feel good about themselves, car parts are hardly sexy. But here's how the magic works: if the UX is as delightful for car parts as it is for swimwear, and the result is that the customer feels their needs have been fully understood and their desire fulfilled to solve a problem at a deeper level, then the webshop is more likely to perform better than if it were simply a functional window display. It goes back to what I wrote earlier – there's a real person at the heart of the decision process to purchase.

According to the consumer theory called 'Jobs to be done'[17] behind every product and service there is a 'job' the customer is trying to complete (i.e. the experience behind the product/service). Once you've identified that experience, you'll also see the main struggles that prevent your customers from achieving it.

Therefore, engage with your potential customers' emotional connection to the product/service by being ahead of the curve to avoid any impediments that prevent them from easily navigating your site in meeting their needs. I cannot overstate the importance of improving emotional connection just as much as any optimised functionality when a webshop aims to transition from start-up to scale up – irrespective of the target market sector.

How you do that is outlined in the following, which is designed to improve the relationship between the store's front and end user.

1. **Speak directly to your customers**

   Discover what excites and frustrates them about their experiences of purchasing online to tailor your webshop copy and marketing content so that it more accurately reflects your service level values and desire to create that delightful UX. After all, you hope to provide them with a service that both resolves their pain points and motivates them to buy. Analyse your best customers to learn which of the motivators are specific or more important.

2. **Focus solely on that experience**

   Let customers know how your product/services allow them to achieve their aims faster, better, cheaper. Do this via written and video content across all channels, including the webshop, social media and marketing activity. This increased sense of emotional connection between you and your customers will reflect positively on your brand and make it more relevant, memorable and impactful.

3. **Continuously ask 'How might we...?' (HMW?)**

    These questions increase emotional connection by showing you value your customers' feedback in how your webshop can improve.

    These should be short, for example:

    - 'How might we make it more fun?'

    - 'How might we make you feel more secure about your purchase?'

4. **Commit to emotional connection as a priority and key lever**

    Not just in the marketing department, but across every function in the business.

As Scott Magids et al. observes:

"Embracing an emotional-connection strategy across the organisation requires deep customer insights, analytical capabilities, and, above all, a managerial commitment to align the organisation with the new way of thinking."[18]

In the article, they contend that customers are emotionally connected with a brand when it aligns with their own motivations and helps them fulfil deep, often unconscious, desires.

Of course, there are a variety of reasons we connect emotionally with a brand. Many of us grew up believing Tide was the greatest laundry detergent because the TV bombarded us with advertisements during *Sesame Street*. You may still use a product or service today because a family member once used it, such as a grandparent who drove a specific car brand. It could be that a parent helped you open a savings account when you were 12 (and you're still with that bank today), or a sugary cereal your aunt gave you when you had a sleepover at your cousin's house.

You may also feel connected to a brand because of a great experience – the airline that upgraded you, or the restaurant with free appetisers. Every organisation has the potential to make a positive impact on someone's life. When a company goes even further and connects with customers' emotions, the pay-off can be huge.

Important emotional motivators include desires to 'stand out from the crowd', 'have confidence in the future', and 'enjoy a sense of well-being', to name a few. To paraphrase Magid's research findings, although brands may be liked or trusted, most fail to align them-selves with the emotions that drive their customers' most profitable behaviours.

I wholeheartedly agree with this sentiment.

CASE STUDY: REVAMPING THE UX FOR AN ENGAGING SHOPPING JOURNEY

Overview

I worked with a lifestyle brand that felt their Woo-Commerce store lacked a captivating user experience, resulting in low customer engagement and a high cart abandonment rate. It was clear to me where the problems lay, primarily in a lack of understanding of their target customers' pain points. In addition, the customer journey was not streamlined, they needed to endure too many clicks to reach the point whereby their problem would be solved – and then they'd buy.

There's never an overnight solution to creating that delightful UX, especially for lifestyle products and services, and so this will always be an incrementally tested process. Sometimes that means webshop owners thinking outside the box a little more, and offering their clients more creative, tailored solutions, such as the online eye wear retailer that would allow customers to select several pairs of glasses so that they could retain which one they preferred and return the ones they didn't. That's not a technological solution, of course, but it is one that complements the webshop's dedication to customer service and a delightful UX. For my particular client, the challenge was to revamp their website's UX/ UI to create a more engaging shopping journey.

Actions Taken

1. User research and feedback gathered to identify pain points and areas of improvement in the user experience.

2. Streamlined the purchasing process by reducing the number of steps required to complete a transaction.

3. Created a visually appealing and intuitive interface with clear product categorisation, easy navigation, and prominent search functionality.

4. Incorporated customer reviews and ratings on product pages to both build trust and to help shoppers make informed decisions.

5. Optimised the mobile experience with responsive design and touch-friendly interactions to cater to the growing number of mobile shoppers.

Outcomes

With a laser-like focus on enhancing the UX/UI, the company witnessed a remarkable transformation in customer engagement. The cart abandonment rate decreased by 30%, while the average order value increased by 20%. Customers enjoyed the intuitive browsing experience and were more likely to complete their purchases, resulting in improved sales and customer satisfaction.

SUMMARY

———————

Understanding what lies underneath the 'hood' of your business's engine will be hugely advantageous in how you continue to shape and evolve your eCommerce business. After all, when you compare what's beneath the hood of a Tesla it will vary considerably to that of a Ford Escort. On the surface, both vehicles will get you from A to B, but your user experience will be vastly different.

Therefore, in respect of your own webshop, imagine what your competitors look like in your customers' eyes, and determine which one of you is an aspirational vehicle, and which is more functional. It's not always a matter of focusing on your products alone, it's about that journey your customers take to get from A to B.

Knowing how and where to solicit constructive criticism and acting upon it in order to raise your webshop's profile, standing and performance is vital, even if at times that critique stings. Turn data into actionable insights that then add value to the business. Not only is that good for the business, but ultimately for customers, too, in enhancing their user experience.

- See the world through your client's eyes. Ask 'what is the user's emotional connection with the brand?'

- UX goes beyond the webshop and requires fundamentally different questions. 'How might we?'

- Your webshop should be delightful to use (rather than just pleasing to the eye).

- It should be both efficient (easy to browse, intuitive, fast) and effective in generating sales or other business results (increased loyalty, faster conversions, etc).

- An important part of improving the Usability and UX on your webshop is to improve the Information Architecture (content organisation, navigation, search and labelling).

- You will know 'you got there' when your clients tell you they are having a delightful experience with your store.

- Relentlessly improve the Usability and UX to allow you to become a remarkable premium brand.

CHAPTER 5

WALK BEFORE YOU CAN RUN FASTER

The next logical step of the Foundations Roadmap is to increase traffic to the webshop. Before I address that, in this chapter I invite you to briefly pause and reflect on where your growth plan strategy is right now. As I mentioned earlier, most leaders in the early stages of a business focus primarily on strategies to generate volume sales in what I contend is the mistaken belief this facilitates those expansion plans.

Obviously, anything that attracts and increases conversions is an important cornerstone of the vision. Nobody would argue against the need for any eCommerce venture to prosper. However, a word of caution: if you're about to greenlight a major marketing campaign, or enter new markets, then be prepared to avoid the common mistakes that many make in the belief they can run before they can walk. This is the right time to ask yourself and your team if you have the requisite foundations in place to either:

- generate that increased traffic
- properly support additional volume traffic with the appropriate infrastructure.

Don't mistake me, I applaud your confidence in your ability to drive future growth, but the first question you should ask yourself before implementing any plan is – will your current platform cope with any significant increase in traffic?

Possibly you've already created, or planned for, a better version of the webshop (either by employing in-house or external freelancers) where the goal is to release product into the marketplace faster. Better still, you may also intend to carry out split testing on your marketing content to see which performs the best, in which case, that's an excellent starting point. However, I've seen far too many webshops fail because they've not ensured that their platform can support the antic- ipated growth. Instead, they pay too much attention to giving it a fantastic aesthetic makeover without any consideration that it may not be able to handle a significant increase in traffic when a major marketing campaign goes live. This is a classic error to be avoided at all costs.

As I've outlined above, the ultimate goal should always be to create a completely delightful UX for customers. That demands a laser-like focus on the elements I've described that ensure the webshop provides a world-class service without falling over when it experiences major functionality and usability issues that result in difficulties for customers and damages its reputation.

To avoid that nightmarish scenario, preparation is key. Central to any big vision is the creation of a framework that offers proper support before any expansion plans go live. On that basis, I suggest you prevent any such crash and burn by following the three preparatory steps below:

1. SEO MASTERY AND ENHANCED ENGAGEMENT

A drip-drip content marketing approach eases your brand into public awareness. It prevents that sudden, damaging rush of traffic to the platform which may not be equipped to handle it. This also helps discover who your market really is. With so many webshops competing for attention, it also reduces the emotional imperative to immediately sell, sell, sell. It also allows your brand to be more creative in attracting new customers using content that will help it stand out from the crowd.

How can that be achieved?

- Publish regular blogs, most commonly known as 'content marketing'. This is extremely effective and hugely popular with US businesses. Blogs help boost SEO quality by positioning your website as a relevant answer to your customers' questions. It's an organic method of growing traffic where results are delivered over a period of time. The more content created containing specific target keywords, the more your web-shop's url is picked up via the search engines, such as Google. The more searches that match your keywords, followed by click-throughs, the higher your brand ranks, which in turn drives more traffic.

It is, however, a waiting game, one that companies must be prepared to invest in. Companies that rec-ognise this contribute incrementally to future growth and assigned larger content delivery teams will get the desired positioning and visibility. As a result, they will generate more revenue and will be able to continue to further optimise, thus leaving their counterparts behind.

The downside (although I don't view it as such) is that it's more difficult to measure those results due to the organic nature and length of time involved. I, therefore, recommend you commit resources to create strategically targeted blogs in order to raise brand awareness. In my opinion it's a wait that reaps rewards.

The alternative approach is to place a series of online ads, or 'paid media'. One clear advantage is that by spending money to promote content, a brand reaches a larger pool of people. That includes those not subscribed to its social media channels that may not even be aware of it. Paid media is a good opportunity to enrich completely new connections. It's also possible to precisely quantify the return on investment over the course of a specific campaign.

Surprisingly, many webshops believe that paid media isn't worth this investment. In one sense, I agree, it's no guarantee of generating leads that then convert, unless the offer is an affordable one that tempts people to buy on impulse. However, I also believe that paid media doesn't always necessarily need to be employed as an overt sales tool. In fact, I'd argue that it's more effective as a means of nurturing customers.

My top tip is, instead of placing a paid for *'this is our product, buy it'* advertisement, try to initially attract attention using some possible connection angle. Think of when you find yourself at a party and want to meet someone you're interested in. It's important to approach the situation with a tactful strategy rather than immediately proposing to 'go out'. Building a connection requires finding an angle that creates a comfortable and engaging atmosphere for both individuals involved. For instance, you can start a conversation by discussing a shared interest, such as a hobby or a topic related to the event or location. This could involve commenting on the music playing in the background, discussing what food has been served up, or even complimenting something unique about the party's atmosphere. By finding a common ground, you create a starting point that can naturally lead to further conversation and rapport. Through genuine and thoughtful engagement, you establish a foundation of mutual understanding and interest, paving the way for a potential future meeting. Taking the time to get to know someone and build a connection gradually allows for a more organic and meaningful relationship to develop. The same applies online.

2. TEST YOUR ADS

Whichever paid media route you choose the only certain outcome is that it will cost. It's surprising, therefore, that many webshops frequently fail to test the effectiveness of their expensive paid for advertising sufficiently enough (if at all).

Ideally, a creative team will produce several small budget content campaigns to then test which performs the best. They'll determine which advert is the real winner with the public because the data supports the result. Without a test process in place, they might as well set fire to their cash. Testing isn't rocket science, but it is accurate when followed through methodically.

How should you test?

- 'Split', (aka A/B testing), involves an 'experimentation' process wherein two or more versions of a web page (or page element) are released into the digital marketplace. This determines which version creates the maximum impact and drives business metrics.

- Split testing allows for the creation of differing versions of the same advert.

- The CTA may vary over time to allow analysis of which one is the most effective.

Bear in mind, not all adverts are about selling, their purpose may be to nurture new customers in the long term. For example, in a split test the CTA may include them signing up for:

Page A

A special offer + download a free pdf booklet.

Page B

A free gift + download a free pdf booklet.

With split test A (your initial variable control page) if 100 people visit the page, but only 10 respond to the CTA, you'd wonder why only 10% clicked through to the next step and then only 1% of the total actually made a purchase (or became a lead).

Perhaps it means that you haven't explained yourself clearly enough, and so, you'd need to evaluate how you could improve on this conversion rate. In which case, you'd return to the copy and take a closer look at the choice of words or flow. You then modify your messaging so that in split test B (the variation of control A) you can move more people along the funnel, squeezing them like a tube of toothpaste, pushing them to the next step.

This process of experimentation generates valuable data insights and eliminates the need for guesswork. However, this journey of discovery should never end: if your page B begins to deliver better results it then becomes the control which can be further tested against another variation, page C and so on.

Page B

A free gift + download a free pdf booklet.

Page C

Invitation to book a free discovery call + download a free pdf booklet.

My best advice – spend your money wisely on incremental split testing, not on a one-time big hitter advert in the first instance, because it simply may not deliver the results you hope for. In which case, you'll be back to square one.

As counterintuitive as it sounds, time is one of your biggest assets because the data you receive from continually rotating your ads and split-testing your hypotheses basis will point you in the right direction.

It will also result in a greater ROI. Traditional marketing is, by its very nature, a much slower method from which to derive analysis from. At one time a business might part with several thousands to place an advert in a single channel print magazine that takes weeks to prepare, then an even longer lag between publication and return on investment.

The digital age, on the other hand, transforms and streamlines those opportunities on multiple levels via which to explore and leverage a whole variety of platforms. It is, without doubt, the game changer.

I hope that you understand me when I say I am continually puzzled when some webshop owners still run untested adverts via traditional mass market print and broadcast channels. Especially as it needn't be an expensive process. For more specialist advice on split testing and marketing techniques, a number of experts[19] are available to guide you.

3. BUILD LINKS AND PARTNERSHIPS

When you create your own media content, I recommend that you widen the scope of people to talk to beyond your own immediate realm. It's far more productive to reach beyond this echo chamber and build links/partnerships that will widen the perspective that then helps your brand speak to a whole new audience:

- Link to top performing channels.

- Solicit an invitation to write a guest post.

- Feature as a guest on a podcast as a meaningful way to generate new awareness for your brand.

Any initiative that builds links back to your webshop will help promote its content on other platforms/channels and increase traffic. Develop strategic partnerships that share the demographic you intend to reach. This is totally 100% acceptable since it allows the brand to 'piggyback' on someone else's success in order to direct users to your own content.

In addition, I suggest that brands make themselves visible on other popular sites and portals such as Reddit, LinkedIn, Quora, SlideShare etc. This is not only effective, it's free. Add your own comments in response to posts where you can make your presence felt. For example, join a discussion about market trends and you'll soon likely see an uptick in activity on your own site.

If nothing else, your visibility and opinions increase your authority with the additional benefit of attracting new people from other communities than your own. As the number of leads increase, so will your confidence in the certainty that your content strategy will reap rewards.

CASE STUDY: OPTIMISING CONVERSION RATES THROUGH A/B TESTING AND PERSONALISATION

Overview

An online home decor store enjoyed a high number of visitors but struggled with low conversion rates on their WooCommerce website. One of the clearest causes I identified was the lack of trust between the store and its customers was very apparent. The site certainly sold products that customers would like, but without testimonials and reviews, they were more cautious in purchasing from this retailer. Stephen Covey articulates the importance of trust excellently in his book in which he contends[20] that the lack of it is the **number one** reason why people won't buy.

A webshop can include as many big, bold 'buy now' buttons all over its pages, but that's never the prime incentive in the customer's mind. In fact, it can have quite the opposite effect and 'buy now' becomes synonymous with 'bypass', especially if it's the first thing a customer sees on the page. 'Buy now' has no inherent story attached to it, there is nothing compelling about its presence in isolation. What this tells me is that the business has focused its attention on the wrong priority first. 'Buy now' has to be backed up with a set of foundations that customers will trust are sound and solid. Because, let's not forget, today's digital consumers are savvy and curious, and they'll do their research on the seller as much as they will on the product in order to then make an informed purchase. And if that can feel like it's more tailored to their needs, the better the chance of conversion.

Therefore, for my client, the aim was to optimise their conversion rates through A/B testing and offer personalised experiences tailored to their customers' preferences.

Actions Taken

1. Identified, through data analysis, pages with high exit rates and potential areas of improvement.

2. Implemented A/B testing for key elements such as call-to-action buttons, page layouts, and product descriptions to identify optimal variations.

3. Increased use of personalised product recommendations based on customers' browsing and purchase history to enhance search relevance and cross-selling opportunities.

4. Employed exit-intent pop-ups with enticing offers or discounts to capture potential customers before they leave the website.

5. Simplified the checkout process by reducing the number of form fields along with guest checkout options.

Outcomes

By optimising its conversion strategies, the webshop witnessed a significant increase in conversion rates. The A/B tests resulted in a 20% improvement in click-through rates and a 15% increase in add-to-cart rates. The personalised experiences led to a 25% increase in average order value. Overall, these improvements translated into higher revenue and improved customer satisfaction.

SUMMARY

Content is still king, paid for or otherwise. However, a word of caution: a sudden wave of significantly increased traffic that then floods your webshop without the necessary preparation (see Chapter 6 for the detail) could undo all of your good work to date.

- Be patient, be smart and build awareness of your brand iteratively.

- Instant success isn't always the ideal objective of paid media content.

- Explore other effective content strategies that help raise awareness of your brand and engage existing subscribers plus potential new leads.

- Test, test, test the processes.

- Every data insight gained will be invaluable, it deepens your understanding of your webshop and also the emotional connections with your customers.

- Finally, never stop testing.

People change, markets come and go, fashions and trends evolve...

... and so must you, if you wish to run faster!

CHAPTER 6

TRAFFIC

So far, I've outlined the importance of laying down the essential foundations every webshop needs in place before implementing plans for future growth, especially in its efforts to attract customers in larger numbers.

I've seen so many clients, following a period of steady growth, try to navigate their mounting sense of frustration as they see their conversion rates plateau. In this chapter, I share additional tools and insights to increase your webshop's capacity and how to handle levels of increased traffic that could see a rise from several thousand orders per week to several thousand **per hour**.

One consistent regret I hear from CEOs is their selection of WordPress as their webshop's platform. They feel deflated because they believe it fails to both handle high volume traffic and fully deliver that much-antici-pated growth. I completely understand that sense of disappointment. You may also feel that way. However, I'd counter that, without the Foundations Roadmap in place, that was always likely to be the outcome. The reality is, WordPress is more than capable and it **can** meet your initial expectations.

Why do I say that? Principally, your biggest WordPress advantage is that **you are in control**. You have the abil-ity to influence, change and stimulate your own growth path because it's your hands that are on the tiller. Add to that, you are already well supported by the requisite resources and expertise inside, and outside, of your business.

On the other hand, webshops hosted by platforms such as Shopify and similar are more reliant on built-in presets and service agreements that limit autonomous decision making. Therefore, the opportunities to influ-ence growth are somewhat restricted.

Compare that with WooCommerce's affordable and relatively powerful web hosting service that enables webshops to tackle their challenges more proactively and, as a result, make those autonomous decisions. However, some webshop owners feel it fails them the moment they run a flash sale.

Why? Because the platform isn't optimised to handle the subsequent and significant increase in traffic. All they witness is a barrage of frustrated customers unable to refresh and load nonfunctional pages that simply don't take them through the whole purchasing process (another undelightful UX to be avoided).

How often have we heard that familiar story of a site that crashes within five minutes of concert tickets being released to market? The answer is, too often, despite the fact I suggest this is an avoidable disaster. Such poor performance only serves to damage the merchant's reputation. In worst case scenarios, this soon becomes a Twitter storm of protest that then gets picked up by the mainstream media.

Even the bigger brands aren't immune from this. In November 2022, singer/songwriter Taylor Swift publicly criticised Ticketmaster for leaving fans waiting in online queues for up to eight hours, with many missing out on pre-sale tickets for her first, much anticipated tour in five years after its website became overwhelmed. Ticketmaster responded by blaming 'extraordinarily high demands on ticketing systems and insufficient remaining ticket inventory to meet that demand.'[21] Swift, in a statement on Instagram, said, 'We asked them, multiple times, if they could handle this kind of demand and we were assured they could.'[22]

With the appropriate planning and foundations in place, this should have been preventable. Similarly, when UK high street fashion retailer Primark launched its first ever online webstore in November 2022, the site also crashed due to 'unexpected' high demand.

I'm puzzled that even today, with a whole variety of sophisticated tools and simple planning strategies available to webshop owners, this type of event continually occurs. Site malfunctions cause customers aggravated frustration that risks them looking to purchase from a competitor site once the seed of desire has been planted in their heads. This is to be avoided at all costs.

The aim is to avoid disaster when a sudden influx of visitors can cause the site to crash as customers rush to purchase in high volumes following that attention-grabbing broadcast TV spot, or social media campaign featuring a high-profile influencer.

Before you agree to greenlight any major marketing campaign, you must first have sight of the whole picture. Whilst it's tempting to rush headlong towards that fantastic entrepreneurial vision where the business grows and scales to the heights you've dreamed of, don't. You'll soon discover it's not always easy to create a masterpiece.

Even Picasso took his time to create his works and, even then, whilst many looked on in awe at his success, others told themselves 'I could've done that!' Replicating or trying to outperform your competitive 'masters' is no easy task. In reality, it took Picasso many, many hours of learning his craft, developing his artistry and understanding of form before he could stretch the boundaries and challenge expectations of the norm. Picasso makes Picasso's brilliance look easy.

The same is true when we look at the biggest and most successful webshop and internet-based brands. Their success follows a logical pathway backed by the requisite infrastructure where it's 'all hands on deck'. As a leader, the fundamentals of entrepreneurship will be natural to you, but I also encourage a greater buy-in to the notion of collective responsibility as opposed to the more prevalent boardroom tendency to delegate. You will recall I've previously mentioned that I regard delegation as an abdication of responsibility.

Traffic isn't simply a one-way street.

CASE STUDY: GROWING TO HIGH WEB TRAFFIC

Overview

A ladies' swimwear brand hosted on WordPress webshop really looked the part – smart, great design layout and high grade, well shot images of the products worn by professional models. The goal behind a high-profile flash sale was to shift as much of the webshop's limited back catalogue that they didn't intend to restock. Unfortunately, the webshop owners didn't have the benefit of the four foundations in place prior to going live with the much-hyped promotion. They created an almost festival fervour that encouraged droves of customers to enter the site almost all at the same time.

As a result, they experienced outages and problems due to high traffic surges that flooded their webshop. This caused the webshop to respond more and more slowly as it tried to accommodate more and more requests from consumers eager to purchase this limited stock supply. Eventually, the burden was too much for the server to handle and the webshop became inaccessible for a few minutes. Once enough people had resigned from the process, the webshop would come up again, at least for a while, until the threshold was reached again. It created an unprofessional experience. At this point, they approached me via WidgiLabs to help them resolve this with the goal of 'scale up to the next level'.

Actions taken

1. The issues they experienced were addressed head on with a view to finding a solution in order to completely reinvent both the webshop and the infrastructure that supported it.

2. Changes to hosting provisions and implementing various upgrades included a revamp of the webshop design, operational and back-office infrastructure adjustments, theme refactoring, plugin audits and custom development to reduce bloat from commercial plugins.

3. The database was fine-tuned and advanced front-end optimisations were tailored to their needs. Unlike out-of-the-box plugins, some of the necessary changes were unique to this specific webshop and the way it had been first assembled.

4. Utilisation of cloud servers to handle increased on demand capacity.

Outcomes

When the webshop's store was relaunched, the client was then able to launch new product catalogues without any of the hiccups it had previously experienced. These improvements, including the capacity to run marketing campaigns that involved Instagram celebrities and major publications enabled it to operate as a high-traffic webshop. The result was that the overall experience for the thousands of consumers simultaneously attempting to make purchases on this webshop was radically smoother. As a result, the client's reputation was enhanced. Additionally, with a subsequent increase in international sales, the client was more confident they could run future large-scale campaigns without worrying about their store's capacity to handle the demand.

It's important to mention that this performance overhaul wasn't the result of a huge increase in infrastructure costs since these were maintained within a fixed monthly budget. The business would, therefore, not be punished each time they were featured by influencers or appearing in TV slots. Many similar webshop owners are tempted to simply throw a lot of money at the problem by adding additional servers to create more capacity. Whilst that is a part-solution, it's more of a wasted effort if the infrastructure and design of the webshop haven't been first addressed.

For my swimwear webshop client, the solution lay in scaling their servers via Cloud technology because its flexibility responds to differing levels of demand across various territories and time zones without putting a strain on infrastructure resources. This can still be a costly exercise if using either of the two main cloud providers, Amazon web services (AWS) or Google Cloud, since this commits the business to a pay per use model. That inevitably costs more (with no cap to it) should a planned influencer/TV spot promotion prove successful. To avoid this unknown variable, we settled on a fixed monthly budget that ultimately didn't punish the business as a result of successful campaigns. After all, that's why so many webshops' visions are predicated on using WordPress or WooCommerce because they want both the flexibility it affords while also avoiding the expenditure in paying service fees to one-stop hosting providers.

SUMMARY

When you run a campaign where an influencer talks enthusiastically about your products, then you'd better be able to handle the resultant high levels of traffic reaching your server. This means futureproofing your capacity – otherwise you will waste that costly marketing/PR opportunity. What was OK when you only had a few visitors isn't OK now you're going for gold. Growth is contingent on the business ensuring it has the appropriate infrastructure in place (which may be considerably different to your current needs).

There are solutions, of course, but not necessarily out of the box, especially as you've opted for independence by using WordPress. Anticipating and finding the right solution will be key to your webshop's future success that matches its ability to attract those levels of traffic in the first place:

• Solutions should never rely on your team's ability to fix things on the fly despite their proven capabilities when operating at lower volumes of traffic.

• Test and implement all the necessary optimisations in advance of running high profile marketing campaigns so that the business is fit to provide lightning-fast solutions to handle the resultant surge in traffic.

- The elasticity in cloud storage supply is a significant contributory factor in accelerating growth.

When you ensure your webshop has sufficient capacity, you enable it to achieve the growth you anticipate. You also better understand that growth can't be guaranteed via organic methods alone. It's equally as important to measure analytics and improve search engine rankings on an ongoing basis. This requires continuous effort so that your webshop is primed to attain higher conversion rates, realise a healthy ROI thanks to achieving its targets and improve investor confidence. This can only be good for the business in both the medium to long term.

CHAPTER 7

EMOTIONAL
CAPITAL

Without a doubt, the digital age has radically changed the way we all shop. Today, habits are driven more by the individual's own habits and preferences, as opposed to the more traditional herd mentality. During the analogue era, if a particular product appeared fashionable or trendy, it was likely to become the 'must have' item. Arguably, potential purchasers were more relaxed and less discriminating about whether they either wanted or needed that 'must have' item. It's an area of human psychology that's been the subject of extensive academic research, some of which I present below. I always find these studies fascinating and illuminating.

Here's a radical thought: forget the need to attract new customers for a moment and instead focus on your existing clients. Until you excel at that there's no point in ramping up your marketing activity with ambitions of scaling-up. If you take your eye off your current customer base and leave it feeling neglected or badly served, then any attempt to attract new customers is a poor use of time and money.

Think of it like you're about to cast a net upon the waters, except that net has to be calibrated to catch all that enter it. If the net is tight enough, it will catch fish both large and small. However, knowing what makes up that catch is as essential as gathering the fish in one place. Once you have them in your sights, you'll realise that they're not all the same – some are bigger than others – and nor do they all swim in the same direction. If you treat them as if they are all the same, then a large number will slip through the net.

In this chapter, I'll show you how to close that net and draw together each of the elements in the Foundations Roadmap that will steer your business towards explosive eCommerce growth. That includes leveraging the power of Google and social media channels via the webshop so that you're fully equipped to both attract new and retain existing customers where it's empowered to maximise the value from each. At the forefront of it, Google has played a key role in marrying human interaction with the digital era, and on that basis, I will summarise the elements I believe are the most useful for webshop owners to understand.

Fortunately, this doesn't require a huge financial investment. Nor does it involve mountains of research since Google has already done much of the heavy lifting, with results that draw some extremely insightful conclusions.

THE CONSUMER 3-STEP PSYCHOLOGY MODEL

Google's research shows that, prior to the digital age, customers typically cycled through a 3-step psychological model related to shopping:

1. The first moment of truth – this begins with a particular stimulus to enter the store and purchase a product.

2. The experience of the product – where customers have purchased their possession and have either a negative or a positive experience.

3. The second moment of truth – when happy customers share their experience with others.

Conventional thinking led us to believe that if businesses spent enough time on each of these steps, they would succeed. However, in the digital age it would be a mistake to jump to early assumptions given that data and analytics today can more accurately pinpoint customers' browsing behaviour in each part of the shopping cycle. Such in-depth analytics were never fully available to bricks and mortar retail.

Recognising that data analytics would shape the future of eCommerce, Google's research scope included 5,000 shoppers across 12 different product categories. Its objective was to interrogate further what influenced shoppers in deciding to convert their browsing into a sale. The results surprised them: respondents said that they preferred to carry out their own detailed research on the items they were interested in and would often compare one or more vendors before deciding to purchase. For example, as far back as 2010 in the USA, the user was likely to visit on average 5 different sources for a particular product, rising to 10 sources by 2011.

This indicates a staggering shift in consumer power. It shows that before completing a purchase US consumers consider their options more deeply before selecting where to spend their money. The research also pointed to the fact that consumers' decisions were also swayed by social media influencers, as well as discussing their options with friends and family.

Google concluded that when it comes to persuading customers to purchase, the traditional '3-step psychological model' needed to be updated to reflect these trends in the digital age with an additional category.

THE ZERO
MOMENT OF TRUTH[23]

The result of this research was a game-changer.

The zero moment of truth is when consumers carry out their own research. They get smart about comparing product alternatives as reassurance that the purchase decision they make will be correct. Google's research discovered that customers actively spend time reading reviews about the products, as well as vendors' reputation and provenance. Consumers also search for online coupons and discounts before deciding to commit to purchase.

Given these are key insights into the psychology that leads to purchasing, the obvious conclusion is that digital marketers should ask themselves the following:

Is their marketing model predicated on an outdated preconception that customers purchase based primarily on visual stimulus alone?

It leaves me wondering if many digital marketers are even aware of the original '3-step psychological model', let alone the 'zero moment of truth'. If not, I'd strongly advise they should be!

It's hardly surprising that the digital era and access to the web has changed shopping into becoming a more nuanced, personalised activity. Of course, high profile online ads and influencer campaigns certainly do drive enormous volumes of traffic to webshops, leading to significant sales uptakes. However, it's also true that the ability to browse more at leisure has enabled users to search (and research) in a more personalised way, meaning that brands are especially keen to exploit personal tastes.

For example, Nespresso successfully developed a range of coffee flavours that align closely to individual consumers' preferences. This tells us that a certain degree of niche marketing tailored to people's needs can increase the probability of success. Nespresso is dedicated to innovation and continually evolves its product offering. Most new flavours are often limited editions, released on a seasonal basis. The goal is to offer customers something new to try when they go to purchase their usual order. This keeps the experience fresh and interesting, which ensures the customer continues to buy from you over a longer period of time.

It's a strategy Nespresso has migrated and refined from its early days of operation in the 1980s, focusing as it does on building its CRM. They've always been well aware that their success would be based on ongoing customer retention and not simply an initial, single purchase order. It also puts its values right into the hands of the consumer through emphasising its sustainability credentials via positive messaging – they pledge to give the world its 'positive cup'. It helps the brand stand out and speak directly to its target market.

For any eCommerce brand the question remains:

How can they then stand out from the competition and funnel those potential customers towards their net?

Despite what some people might say, it's not an art – it's a science. It requires a net that's just tight enough to catch the target users in their flow, populated with products that make customers feel better about what it is they're buying. And often, it's up to you, the webshop owner, to point them in the right direction. Here's how.

BUILD A COMPLETE BUYER PERSONA

First things first – always remain people focused.

There's no excuse these days for any digital business to not interrogate data generated by their customers and spend some time walking in their customers' shoes. There's also a staggering array of online tools at a webshop's disposal offering multiple possibilities to:

- inspect how people use their sites

- learn how users navigate their sites

- find out where they spend time reading information, how long they linger on certain pages and where they get blocked.

With every new discovery, you'll understand what stimulates customers beyond the design visuals and what triggers them to purchase. Remember to:

- be imaginative, empathetic and aligned

- leverage the power of scarcity and build urgency in needing to make a purchase.

For example, if your webshop is open 24 hours a day and filled with a seemingly infinite amount of stock, there's no impulse to buy. The ladies' swimwear client I referred to previously already knew how to leverage the power of scarcity, they simply lacked the proper planning and infrastructure before they went live with their flash sale. However, the scarcity principle was excellent, and once they had rectified their mistakes, they increased that sense of customer excitement by adding a countdown clock to when the 'doors' would open for the sale. It's not such a new idea, they borrowed and adapted it from the large bricks and mortar retailers that had once been famous for enticing long lines of people to queue around the block prior to their big end of year sales.

With the right pieces of the eCommerce puzzle in place, online stores can easily replicate that sense of customer excitement, even on a weekly basis. Once customers become used to the ordering cycle, then knowing they might miss the flash sale deadline, they'll not want to wait another week. My fresh fruit and vegetable webshop client (see the case study below) adopted this as a successful sales attractor, and it works! Flash sales of limited stock or a weekly cycle are both very valid techniques that webshops of any size can leverage to their advantage where the customer feels like they are winning.

Apple Inc. are adept at this practice. They regularly release new variants of the iPhone where each generation includes a newly added or updated feature. Customers loyal to the brand are even prepared to pay a subscription. In effect, they rent the latest model until the next version appears on the market. Apple has been super successful in honing that tension between supply and demand.

The good news is that you don't have to be an Apple Inc to achieve similar results. The additional advantage is that, as a smaller enterprise, you can both engage with and respond to customer needs more quickly on account of not holding huge warehouses of infinite stock. Almost overnight you have the flexibility t o change a strategic plan or activity if required. Thankfully, you're not constricted by the rules of scale that the likes of Amazon are and so it's more feasible to ship a trial case of 10 different p airs o f g lasses t o a customer on a 'try before you buy' basis. For an online giant, that would be a nightmare.

TEST CONTINUOUSLY

Learn from the online behemoths, such as Google, Facebook, Airbnb, and test, test, test!

These online megastars leverage data extensively and continually learn from user behaviour. They implement small, incremental changes as a result of split testing, sometimes up to 100 times during the course of a single day. The impact of one of those small improvements can be hugely significant because it helps webshop owners better understand customer behaviours and preferences in acute detail, for example:

- Do they want to subscribe immediately?

- Do they require more information?

- What actually works best for them?

The more a webshop tests, the more it understands how to plan and execute its call-to-action strategies.

I strongly advocate the need to invest in testing, to mine the data and gain incredible insights into your customers via the analytics generated. Rushing headlong into market without testing when the expressed intent is to only generate high volume sales will rarely deliver, or sustain, in the long term.

BRING IN THE EXPERTS

We all need mentors and partners.

When Airbnb's founders wanted to learn why rental properties in New York (their most searched for destination) failed to convert into as many reservations as they expected, they hired in a consultant, Paul Graham. Together they visited the NYC listings in person to discover why some performed better than others.

They learned that the listings that published high res, professional images were the ones that converted into actual sales. Their solution was to provide professional photography for all their NYC listings. Within a short period of time, they could measure the direct correlation between the pro photography properties and an increase in revenue.

However, to their surprise, revenue soon plateaued. Once again, they needed to discover the cause behind this. Their answer was as simple as could be – the photographer they'd hired was too busy to commit to the entire job and so he was released. They hired a more readily available photographer to capture a higher volume of properties, and before too long, their revenue increased.

The learning here is that expert partners can help you reach new milestones. That's because their impartiality allows them to view the whole landscape from a distance. Often, partners and/or mentors are the ones on your 'team' that help you understand your webshop's entire picture. Integrate them into your plans for future expansion; it's a good investment between stagnation and growth.

External party professionals whose expertise has been put to good use multiple times, help identify where specific problems have either been overlooked or not prioritised. It's the small two-millimetre changes and their insights that can make all the difference to a business.

CASE STUDY: FROM OBSCURITY TO OPPORTUNITY – ELEVATING SALES WITH A SUSTAINABILITY NARRATIVE

My client, a fresh fruit and vegetable vendor, was keen to increase sales. Initially their online story was opaque and unengaging to the extent they were consequently losing custom to larger, more generic, vendors.

I quickly identified a key component of their story that simply wasn't being told: that sustainability was their USP.

Once this was trumpeted on their site, customers started to sit up and take more notice. They were attracted to the fact that their product was fresh, harvested directly from the land and sold directly to the customer. Not only that, the products were healthy and full of flavour.

Once the sustainability information was included into their story, it drove their revenue significantly higher because their target market was niche and affluent. In this respect, the webshop was able to out-perform its bigger retail competitors.

Our client's learning was that they were in complete alignment with their customers' values and mindset; as a result, they were able to sell a sense of happiness with every transaction.

SUMMARY

Investing emotional capital in your business is worth its weight in gold.

Every webshop that plans to grow and scale seriously needs to invest as much in emotional capital as it does in its website's technical functionality. This is about embracing the ultimate optimisation of both human and technical resources in areas where you, as a leader, are involved in all strategic planning and decision-making elements to help the business pivot and grow. Only now can you properly focus on knowing your customers and how their online shopping occurs.

Always be aware that the solutions you seek may not simply be in response to a technical issue. The key point to focus on, as a first point of reference, is that your webshop is people facing, it's run by people, for other people.

Be aware that your customers' journey has changed in the digital era:

- They are choosier and more curious.

- They like to read up about the product.

- They probably prefer to see images of people using the product in different situations before committing to purchase.

The digital shopping landscape sits within that people environment. I assume your goal is for your eCommerce business to explode and reach new heights. Therefore, invest the time and resources into your emotional capital so that you understand the psychology behind the customer's shopping experience.

- Invest in testing.

- Mine the data and gain incredible insights into your customers via the analytics generated.

- Interrogate the data and take time to learn how users navigate the site.

- Discover where customers spend time reading information and how long they linger on certain pages.

- Leverage the power of scarcity and build urgency.

- Call in expert partners – they can help you reach new milestones.

CONCLUSION

One of the reasons you picked up this book is because you run a successful eCommerce business, most probably hosted by WordPress. You may also have been frustrated to date by the fact your webshop's sales have recently plateaued and you're eager to fulfil your entrepreneurial vision to see the business grow and scale.

You made a conscious decision to select WordPress because it's seemingly more adaptable to your needs and is less expensive than using a third-party application, such as Shopify. Far from being limited by third-party partners, you value the real autonomy that WordPress offers, but recently, the business seems to have hit a brick wall. Success is your goal, and yet you've lacked the clarity and expertise to make that an explosive reality. Until now, you may have even questioned your platform hosting decision to host your webshop on a WordPress or WooCommerce platform.

Reading this book has, I hope, offered you both reassurance and a sense of security in knowing that your initial instinct was correct. Explosive eCommerce success is perfectly feasible when you are the one in control. I'd suggest that, until now, it's not been possible to fully identify the issues that have held your growth plans back.

By now you should feel more confident to involve yourself in the necessary conversations you've either shied away from or delegated to others. This book shows that you can lead on all levels whilst still deferring to others' expertise. Asking the right questions is just as important as knowing all the answers. In fact, I'd say more so, because asking the wrong questions leads to a tailspin of wrong answers and assumptions.

Once you master the Foundations Roadmap, you and your team will be aligned and prepared to implement any necessary changes correctly. Understanding each individual stage in its complexity is not as important for you as is understanding the principles of the Roadmap in its entirety. Once it's accepted that this is a collaborative effort, that's when the real magic occurs.

I've already advised you that in the early stages you'll confront an array of uncomfortable issues that will feel a little overwhelming. At times on your journey, it might seem that nothing's working, but trust me when I say that you should stick with the plan. It will deliver. This process requires total commitment. Scaling up an eCommerce business takes dedication, blood, sweat and tears. It is no easy task and requires no less than a complete system, such as the one I've presented in this book. Even if you achieve only 80% of what I've outlined throughout this book, I can guarantee you'll still have created an impactful, successful and functioning webshop.

Therefore, I hope that the Foundations Roadmap offers the logical guidance and insights to help look objectively inside your business in order to reignite, or even kick start, that planned for growth trajectory. I also hope it's prompted you to interrogate how your webshop can serve the real needs of your customers and if it's aligned to their values. Trust and empathy are key drivers in earning their loyalty. I won't pretend, it won't always be plain sailing. For sure, there will be times when you feel frustrated that progress feels slow. That's natural, since the results of your efforts won't always show up immediately. It will take time, and some elements will take longer than others. Stay the course, follow the logical order as I set out. Don't be tempted to rush to increase your conversion rates ahead of the previous steps I've described.

Managing an eCommerce business is never complete or guaranteed to be a success unless you put the work in. It requires nurturing, care and a regularly maintained routine. You, your customers and the marketplace will continue to evolve. Your challenge is to decide which new developments or trends align with the greater good of your company, and which don't.

I like to believe that this book answers many of your pressing and persistent questions by raising your awareness of what's required to be in place before you can achieve that explosive eCommerce growth. I hope that now I've laid out the foundations in the form of an ordered pathway, you'll see your way ahead to making that success a reality.

This book began with the premise that, whether consciously or unconsciously, successful eCommerce owners are strong in any one (or more) of the areas I've outlined. The Foundations Roadmap's structure offers that refreshing 360-degree perspective that allows you to continue to develop and build a world-class webshop. It may even become a lighthouse for others in the industry.

There's never been a better time to recalibrate and prepare for your future growth than now. If at any time you get stuck, don't hesitate to reach out for help. I hope you're excited about the journey ahead. I know I am.

LET'S CONNECT

CELL

(+351) 800 500 969

LINKEDIN

www.linkedin.com/in/nunomorgadinho/

EMAIL

nuno@widgilabs.com

WEB

https://www.widgilabs.com

TWITTER/X

https://x.com/morgadin

ENDNOTES

1 If you haven't sold anything online yet a tiny goal that will change your life is this: Make $1 on the internet.

2 Chaffey, Dave. *Digital Business and E-Commerce Management: Strategy, Implementation and Practice*. 6. ed, Pearson, 2015.

3 That isn't to say there aren't other gaps/problems/questions/important areas in eCommerce you may need to look into that are more important for your specific business.

4 If you are curious about this topic, please see my blog post where I share resources and tools you can use to navigate vendors in the marketplace.

5 One of the basic foundations your webshop needs to have is secure HTTPS hosting (the padlock on your browser tab). This requires an SSL certificate, that ensures that the communication between your users and your webshop is encrypted and thus less subject to being hijacked. It's also a must-have for your marketing, because Google penalises webshops with HTTP in organic search rankings.

6 Securi, 2019 Website Threat Research Report.

7 According to data researched by W3Techs, January.

8 A term created by software developer Ward Cunningham, known for being a contributing author of the *Agile Manifesto*, and also for inventing the wiki.

9 Marie Kondo, *The Life-Changing Magic of Tidying Up,* Vermilion, January 2019.

10 A strong password contains at least ten characters comprising upper and lowercase letters, numbers and symbols.

11 When you enable two-step authentication with mobile phones, user accounts become more protected (the password is no longer the only step) but now users have the extra step of having to look at their phones before they can log in.

12 Google has created a tool, PageSpeed Insights, where websites can see how they are ranked and scored in terms of performance. The PageSpeed Score ranges from 0 to 100 points, and a higher score is better and a score of 85 or above indicates that the page is performing well. The report page gives you a useful breakdown of the steps you can take to improve performance. PageSpeed Insights also provides you with additional user experience suggestions for mobile devices.

13 https://www.widgilabs.com/blog/the-importance-of-delightful-ux/

14 Thomas O. Jones and W. Earl Sasser, Jr., *Why Satisfied Customers Defect,* Harvard Business Review, Nov-Dec 1995.

15 Hotjar, https://www.hotjar.com/blog/reduce-ecommerce-bounce-rate/

16 Surveys should be simple and easy for users to complete. Don't exacerbate their frustrations any more than they already are. For a generic sample survey that you can tailor to your needs, follow this link. https://bit.ly/bh-popupsurvey

17 As opposed to 'disruption theory' the 'jobs-to-be-done' theory tells you how to create products and services that customers want to buy, helping us understand customer choice. Data on its own fails to inform us of the causal driver behind a purchase.

18 Scott Magids, Alan Zorfas and Daniel Leemon, *The New Science of Customer Emotions,* Harvard Business Review, Nov 2015.

19 For the most up to date recommended list of providers visit https://cxl.com/blog/ab-testing-tools/

20 Stephen Covey, *The Speed of Trust: The One Thing That Changes Everything,* Free Press, February 2008.

21 Ticketmaster, *Twitter,* November 17, 2022.

22 Taylor Swift, *Instagram Story*, November 18, 2022.

23 Jim Lecinski, ZM, *Winning the Zero Moment of Truth*, Google e-book download, June 2011.